Witchcraft and Self Care

3 Books in 1

How to Communicate with Your Spirit Guide, Powerful
Hoodoo Spells, and Shadow Work for Self-Discovery

Layla Moon

Table of Contents

4 FREE Gifts

To help you along your spiritual journey, I've created 4 FREE bonus eBooks.

You can get instant access by signing up to my email newsletter below.

On top of the 4 free books, you will also receive weekly tips along with free book giveaways, discounts, and so much more.

All of these bonuses are 100% free with no strings attached. You don't need to provide any personal information except your email address.

To get your bonus, go to:

https://dreamlifepress.com/four-free-gifts

Spirit Guides for Beginners: How to Hear the Universe's Call and Communicate with Your Spirit Guide and Guardian Angels

Guided by Moon herself, inspired by her own experiences and knowledge that has been passed down by hundreds of generations for thousands of years, you'll discover everything you need to know to;

- Understanding what the call of the universe is

- How to hear and comprehend it

- Knowing who and what your spirit guides and guardian angels are

- Learning how to connect, start a conversation, and listen to your guides

- How to manifest your dreams with the help of the cosmic source

- Learning how to start living the life you want to live

- And so much more…

Law of Attraction: Manifest Your Desire

Learn how to tap into the infinite power of the universe and manifest everything you want in life.

Includes:

- Law of Attraction: Manifest Your Desire ebook

- Law of Attraction Workbook

- Cheat sheets and checklists so make sure you're on the right path

Hoodoo Book of Spells for Beginners: Easy and effective Rootwork, Conjuring, and Protection Spells for Healing and Prosperity

Harness the power of one of the greatest magics. Hoodoo is a powerful force ideal for holding negativity at bay, promoting positivity in all areas in your life, offering protection to the things you love, and ultimately taking control of your destiny.

Inside, you will discover:

- How to get started with Hoodoo in your day-to-day life

- How to use conjuration spells to manifest the life you want to live

- How casting protection spells can help you withstand the toughest of times

- Break cycles of bad luck and promote good fortune throughout your life

- Hoodoo to encourage prosperity and financial stability

- How to heal using Hoodoo magic, both short-term and long-term traumas and troubles

- Remove curses and banish pain, suffering, and negativity from your life

- And so much more…

Book of Shadows

A printable PDF to support you in your spiritual transformation.

Within the pages, you will find:

- Potion and tinctures tracking sheet

- Essential oils log pages

- Herbs log pages

- Magical rituals and spiritual body goals checklist

- Tarot reading spread sheets

- Weekly moon and planetary cycle tracker

- And so much more

Get all the resources for FREE by visiting the link below

https://dreamlifepress.com/four-free-gifts

BOOK #1

Spirit Guides for Beginners

How to Hear the Universe's Call and Communicate with Your Spirit Guide and Guardian Angels

Introduction

I have felt the presence of spirit guides and the slightly pulling tides of the universe on my physical and spiritual being all my life, but it's only been over the last decade that I've been in touch with this part of myself.

When I was 22 years old, I went through a terrible breakup. Like most of us who go through somewhat bad relationships, especially at a younger age when we don't know any better, I couldn't believe it was happening to me.

The relationship started well, with dates and some fond memories together, but things quickly took a turn for the worst. He would drink a lot, and there were a lot of areas of his life he wasn't happy about - like his career, his financial situation, and his relationships with his friends and family. Being young and naive, I thought we were in love and that our love for each other could save him.

It got worse. One time, my partner lost his job in a rather explosive way, finding the remedy in the bottom of a bottle. Weeks of unemployment turned to months and nearly a year. Throughout this time, the arguments become worse. Day to day life became increasingly violent.

I tried everything to help him out of this dark time and back onto his feet, but I couldn't. I wasn't perfect; of course, I wasn't. I am but only a human. I tried my best, but it wasn't enough.

One night, he left the apartment and slammed the door behind him, leaving me in a cold silence that seemed to last forever. I cried. I cried a lot, and I'm not ashamed of this. I sat with my back against the chair, watching my tears roll down and off my face before the carpet I sat on soaked them up.

That's when I heard it. A voice. It was nothing more than a whisper. At first, I thought the door had been left open, or it was wind coming through an open window, but it wasn't. Even in my vulnerable, defeated state, I could tell it was something more. The atmosphere in the room has shifted so much I couldn't ignore it. I listened closely and just embraced what must be the wind as a welcome chill. But a chill it was not.

It was warm. Friendly. Even inviting. As I felt the hairs on my arm stand on end, I listened, and the soft breeze turned to whispers.

"You need to be free. From this relationship. This experience. This situation. It doesn't serve you."

And the voice disappeared.

At the time, I thought I was going mad. I managed to remind myself I was sad and stressed, and if I was to hear something, even just an unnaturally clear thought, then yes, it was probably to be expected, especially with how I felt. But I couldn't shake the idea that it was something more.

And I was right. Over the next few weeks, I dived into my research, trying to find out what the voice and the whisper could have meant, and very quickly, I stumbled upon the idea of the universe communicating with me. My spirit guides were revealing themselves to me.

Now, this is not a new idea to me.

I have always considered myself a spiritual person and one who consciously, from time to time, connects with the ebbs and flows of the universe, but it wasn't until this moment that it felt so personal. My parents had both been religious, albeit they had been Jehovah's Witnesses. While they believed in God (me not so much), they still dabbled in the ideas of being guided by a more powerful, omnipotent external force.

The forces of the universe, as it were. Now I was experiencing it in real-time.

Over the years, I sought to open my mind and soul, allowing myself to reconnect with these guides, these spirits, and these external forces of the universe. I found a way. Through my career as a writer, spiritual teacher, and practitioner, I have honed my skills and found many ways to open this connection to the universe and my spirit guides. Lessons that anybody can pick up and use for the same results.

These guides have helped to light my path through the brightest and darkest times of my life, offering advice, insight, and clarity whenever I've needed it. Life can be challenging, confusing, problematic, and stressful, and it's always a struggle to know what to focus on and where your mind should be. Fortunately, the guidance from my spirit guides and the universe has helped immensely.

In hindsight, there were plenty of times when my spirit guides communicated with me and sent me signs. They've been there since the day I was born (some even before that) and have shown me the way, even if I haven't realized it in that moment.

The more people I've talked to about this topic, the more firmly I believe the presence of spirits, universal guides, angel numbers, and guardian angels is a kind of magic that everyone has experienced at some point in their lives.

Think back to times in your life where you've had a sudden awakening, a gentle nudge in a new direction, or a much more intense, vivid experience. Maybe you've had a startling realization, or even physically seen your spirit guide manifesting themselves in your presence.

It's not unheard of. It's actually relatively common, but many people write it off as a one-off moment of madness or an inevitable clarity on a given situation. It's not. You can literally manifest these experiences any time you need them, and you can open yourself up to even more opportunities.

Throughout this short book, I aim to provide you with an excellent introductory insight into what it means to connect and open yourself up to the messages, communications, and guidance from both the universe and your spirit guides. We'll explore what this all means, how it works, and how you can introduce these practices into your life, helping you nurture your own connection to your sources of power.

This is how to hear the universe's call and get in touch with the entities that are greater than yourself.

CHAPTER ONE

The Universe is Calling You

"The cosmos is within us. We are made of star-stuff. We are a way for the universe to know itself."

I'm going to split this book into two parts. In the first part, we'll dive into the depths of listening to and tuning into signs from the universe, exploring what they are and how you can connect with them. The second part is dedicated to connecting with your guardian angels and other spirit guides.

Let us begin with the universe.

Many believe the universe is the entirety of space - a boundless place that holds planets, stars, and all the life we know and don't know about. In reality, the universe is home to so much more. As human beings, being in the universe means that you are a part of the universe. The universe is the universe. If you and I are a part of the universe, then we are the same, or at least we come from the same place. We come from the same source and are made of the same energy.

In essence, given the fact that we can feel emotions and witness experiences, many believe that the universe is experiencing itself through humankind. This may feel like a lot to process and understand. It is a complicated idea, and if you're new to it, then yes, it will take more than a few moments to wrap your head around. It's one of those ideas you can comprehend now, but there will be moments of clarity in the future where this concept really hits home.

However, once you start to understand the concept and feel it, a deeper part of you becomes aware that the universe is working in your favor. After all, the universe is you, and you are the universe. Therefore, it's in your best interest to succeed in what you want to do and the kind of life experience you want to have.

Humankind has been around for a long time, and we've evolved so much in a relatively short period, especially considering that the universe is billions of years old, and who knows what happened before that.

During our existence, at least in the forms we know it, our history is laced with stories, myths, and legends about how humans used to be so connected to the Earth and the spirit realm. We worship the sky and meditate on the world's wonders, manifesting some of the most profound beliefs; beliefs that remain relevant in our everyday lives.

If you've ever had the chance to read a religious scripture like the Tao Te Ching, then you know just how powerful these ancient insights can be.

These scriptures and ways of thinking only exist because humans were able to live in harmony with the rest of the universe. There was peace and balance in what we did and the decisions we made. We lived with the nature surrounding us, taking only what we needed and living with respect for the greater powers.

However, there's p little doubt in anyone's mind that we've drifted away this way of living. We now surround ourselves with all things human, from our buildings to our culture, and we see ourselves as the apex of creation. Humans are the be-all and end-all. Or so many of us think.

The judgments and minds of most people are clouded these days. Many of us value things like money and power (human creations) above all else. Others value status or material belongings, but many people want to return to a more balanced, peaceful, and spiritual way of living. This shift in focus towards the material world has taken place over many thousands of years, and it's not something we can simply undo.

It's practically impossible for us to go back to a time before money or before technology, at least not in our mortal lifetimes. Progress is simply unstoppable at this point. However, that's not to say we can't adjust the way we live our lives and the way we think. To do this, you must open your mind to the universe's call.

That you're reading this book means you've already had an experience. It may be small, like hearing an inkling or experiencing a surreal idea pop into your mind that's stuck with you and left you feeling quite strangely about how such an idea was able to appear.

Perhaps you've heard a whisper in the back of your mind that's made you want to learn more and has led you in your research, thus finding this book and this way of thinking. Perhaps your experience was big. Perhaps it was so life-changing, and now you can't go back. You don't have a choice, and you've been placed onto this path, and now you're trying to find your way.

Perhaps you've seen the same set of numbers over and over again, from a bus number, the same sequence appearing in a phone number, to numbers on a clock. No matter where you go, you just can't help but see these numbers repeatedly.

Regardless of your reasons for setting out on this journey, you're here now, which is all that matters.

But how do you know the universe is calling you?

This is a question I asked myself for a long time. During my own experience, I had all these new urges, almost whispers in my head. I can't lie, I was scared. I subtly convinced myself that if I was going mad or had finally lost the plot, I wouldn't be questioning it.

Maybe this was just my own personal growth? Maybe some repressed or dormant part of me was waking up? While I had a shimmer of an idea that the universe was reaching out to me, how could I be sure?

How can *you* be sure?

As we'll discuss in the following chapter, there are signs to look out for, signs that once you start to notice, you can begin to confirm the universe is making itself known to you. I'm a firm believer that this is a process every human being on the planet goes through. It happens when the time is right and when the stars align, but it's up to you to listen to the call or not.

I'm sure you know people in your life who have heard a call to do something or to change or grow somehow, but they've chosen to ignore the call or ignored it unintentionally. This is when people end up in a rut for years, or they just seem bitter. They may get a chance to hear the call again, but it's never certain.

As much as you may love these people, you possess a deep-rooted instinct that leads you to believe who has and hasn't answered their calls and seen the signs. So again, how can you be sure you've heard yours?

How Do You Know You've Heard the Call?

While seeing the signs is a good indication that the universe is calling out to you, other telltale signs help you confirm what you've heard, indicating that it's time to act. When you're living your life day by day in a state of difficulty and frustration, you are not living what you would call 'your best life,' for lack of a better term.

You are living in a state of toleration. You might be in a job you hate, a financial position that frustrates you, or living with someone you don't want in your life. You feel as though you have no choice in the matter. This is just how your life is, and so, you tolerate your living conditions. Oftentimes, most people aren't even aware that this is how they're living. They have just become accustomed to their comfort zone.

To hear the call is to feel a shift within yourself. A change. A new way of thinking. Many say they feel a door open within them, and new opportunities appear to them. It may start small and subtle or loud and obvious. Ever woken up and just felt different? Like you've burst with a new surge of motivation and focus? Have you ever struggled with something, and suddenly, seemingly out of the blue, an answer revealed itself to you?

These are the calls of the universe. However, it's at this moment where most people fall short. I have. You have. Whether it comes as a universal call or an increase in vibrational energy, a lot of people think (or at least wish) that this was enough to make the change. It's not. The cosmic force that governs all doesn't work in this way. If only it were that easy, some might say.

A shift in focus or a raise in vibrational energy, an inner calling from the universal power source, does not change anything. That's on you. To hear a call is one thing. To heed the message itself and then act is another. It's a step-by-step process.

In the next chapter, we'll go through some of the ways the universe contacts human beings, but for now, note that if you notice one or more of these signs, pay extra attention to other possible signs that may come your way. It's through acknowledging these signs that you can hear the call.

Once you know what the signs are, it will be easier to know what you're looking for, but for now, open your awareness as much as you can. Keep your eyes and ears open. Open your mind and your soul. The signs are there.

CHAPTER TWO

Reading the Signs from The Universe

"The universe speaks if you will learn to listen."
— David Bowers

With your mind open and your being starting to accept potential signs the universe may send your way, it's time to begin recognizing what they are. Signs come in shapes, sizes, and methods, but they tend to follow patterns and styles caused by vibrational manifestations.

Allow me to explain,.

Synchronicity

A few years back, my friend was in a similarly challenging relationship as mine, planning to settle down with an abusive partner. From the outside, it was heartbreaking to watch as she repeatedly denied that anything was wrong.

Whenever we met up and she had a new bruise, mark, or broken state of mind, she would always deflect my questions when I asked if she was okay and would remain adamant that things were slowly working out. From the outside, it was clear things were only getting worse.

One week was particularly bad, and my friend was broken, physically and emotionally. It was harrowing to see her in such a state, but still, she refused help. We met for lunch one afternoon, and I couldn't hold back. I dove into how painful it was to see her so broken; and how seeing her so defeated yet staying where she was literally broke my heart.

As we were speaking, a couple was arguing in the café queue about money. The man called his partner a bitch for not having enough cash, and now he had to pay with his card. He overreacted to the situation, causing heads to turn. My friend watched, stunned as we had literally been chatting about a similar situation, yet she pushed it down and changed the subject.

A few nights later, as her partner was working a night shift, I wanted to get her out of the house, so I took her to my book club. She was shy and took her time opening up. The club was held in a small bookstore downtown, and we started by rearranging the chairs into a circle in the main room.

As we moved the chairs around, my friend's chair knocked one of the bookshelves, causing a book to drop from a high shelf. The book that landed in her chair was about overcoming the effects of an abusive relationship and relearning how to love yourself.

My friend cried. She cried her eyes out. We sat outside on a bench as she shared what she'd been noticing over the past two weeks. From the cafe to the book falling into her chair, from seeing TV shows and YouTube videos on abusive relationships, and overhearing other peoples' conversations, she described how it felt like she couldn't escape the topic of abusive relationships.

This is the power of synchronicity.

The universe is a responsive and intricate thing that ebbs and flows with time and experience. Beyond what we can see and comprehend, there are infinite connections between events, words spoken and time, and everything we can't possibly know. This is the impact of the butterfly effect. Even the most minor event can have the biggest impact, and when you start considering the impact of vibrational energies, this effect is magnified tenfold.

Synchronicity is the process of related events that don't seem to abide by the strict laws of cause-and-effect. They are simply messages that come to you in various forms but are so meaningful and impactful in your mind that you can't help but notice them. You've probably had seemingly strange experiences like this in the past.

That was a sign from the universe.

From here on out, keep your eyes open for signs of synchronicity. They can happen anywhere at any time, and they may occur over a day, or even several weeks or months. Synchronicity ties in beautifully with angel numbers because if you start seeing numbers linking up with a certain message, you know a message is coming your way.

Either way, it doesn't really matter how these signs come to you, the most important thing to remember is that they'll stand out, and it's your acknowledgment that means you hear a sign.

Spotting Angel Numbers

If you've ever found yourself seeing the same numbers or patterns of numbers repeatedly, these are signs you should not ignore. In fact, these are one of the most powerful signs the universe can send you, which is why they are known as 'angel numbers.' Angel numbers have been a big part of my life for many years.

For many years, especially while I was in education trying to find the motivation to write my book - and currently from time to time - I always seemed to see the numbers 911, always in that order. Most days, I'd see the time 9:11 both in the morning and evening. I'd see it on car registration plates, at the end of email addresses, and so on.

Due to a large world-changing event, I thought this is just the case. Just an awareness of a dark day, but after taking time to research the spiritual world, I soon realized it was so much more. These were my angel numbers with their own meaning and purpose, and once I started to embrace this meaning and purpose, my life started to change. After all, you're reading this book right now. I made it happen, and the universe helped.

I'll talk about this more later, but for now, just bear in mind that angel numbers exist, and they're important when it comes to helping you connect to the universe, your spirit guides, and ultimately finding your way.

Dreams and Visions

I'll quickly touch on dreams and visions because they are so important when connecting with the universe, and you've probably heard about them before. The messages you hear in your dreams are messages from your unconscious mind, coming to you involuntarily in powerfully visual ways.

Not all dreams will have powerful meanings that will change your life, but if you have a dream that sticks with you for some time, meaning you go through your day with its echo following you, this is a sure sign that you need to dive into that dream to find out what it's trying to tell you.

Fortunately, reading into your dreams and their meanings is easier than ever before, especially with the wide collection of online information.

Deja Vu

Personally, and perhaps a little more lightheartedly, experiencing Deja Vu is one of my favorite signs from the universe because it's so apparent, and it's such an interesting feeling. It can feel so intense, so much so that it's unmistakable. If you experience Deja Vu,   it's time to focus and look for the signs.

Whatever the situation is, take notice of what's happening and the highlight events. What's the topic of conversation you think you've heard before? Who is involved? What are the critical components of what's happening? Even if a pet or a meal or a time of day is standing out to you, pay attention and think about them.

If you can pay attention to the details, you're learning something that can help you in some aspects of your life.

Gut Instincts

Gut instincts or truly sudden emotions don't happen randomly without cause, rhythm, or reason. They have a message to tell you. Sure, it can be hard to interpret these feelings and emotions. Say you were up on stage to talk to a large crowd of people; you may feel hot, prickly, and have a profoundly uneasy feeling in your stomach.

Your first point of call may be to say you're nervous, but notice how these are the exact same emotions and feelings you'd have if you were excited. There's a very thin line between the two. No matter what situation you find yourself in, if you find a sudden emotion consuming you, a message within you starts screaming; you are not losing the plot.

Instead, you are tuning into your intuition and inner insight. For too long, you've probably ignored this part of your being, except on rare occasions, which is why it can feel quite intense when you start allowing it to happen and you start listening to it. Whatever the situation, it exists to tell you something.

The Appearance of People or Animals

One of the final signs you'll want to look out for comes in the form of people or animals. People come and go from our lives all the time, but have you ever noticed how some people seem to come into your life at specific points of your life and then disappear.

Whether they're in your life for a single chance encounter, or for months or years, some people will come into your life to teach you something you need to know or to open your mind to a new way of thinking. This is the universe at work, and usually, probably without even knowing it, you'll be doing the same in their life.

If you meet someone and you get a strange feeling, like an automatic drive to think about a person, such as a lingering feeling that sticks with you after you've met someone, then the chances are they have been introduced to you for a reason. Always try to take note of the feelings you have around people and let their energy in if your instinct tells you to.

The same can apply to the introduction of animals. We'll talk about this more in the next chapter, but if you see animals popping up throughout your life, mainly if they appear in strange places, this could be a sign from the universe. This is even more so the case if you've identified what your spirit animal is.

You just need to keep your eyes open for what animals appear to you during the hardest, strangest, coincidental, or particular times in your life. If you see a pattern, it's likely that the universe is reaching out to you.

All of these are signs to look out for as you go throughout your life. Sometimes you may have an individual, isolated circumstance where you notice something dramatic, or you may experience a series of events that back each other up, become meaningful coincidences, and are practically signs you can't ignore.

It doesn't matter how the universe calls out to you, be open to the signs. Trust your unconscious mind, and when you have an instinct about something, or you feel the first burning sparks of a message or feeling starting to appear within you, it's undoubtedly the universe contacting you. This means it's time for you to listen.

CHAPTER THREE

Spirit Guides and Guardian Angels

"Our spirit whispers are the best guides. And they are found in the very personal, quiet moments when we are doing nothing."
— Jeanne McElvaney.

Building on the previous chapter, precisely the final point, it's time to talk about spirit guides and guardian angels. Sometimes, a sign from the universe is not enough, and a little direct intervention is needed. For better or for worse, you may not be seeing the signs, or perhaps the call you need to hear is coming from a specific place.

This could come from an ancestor or a relative. It could come from someone you've never met, or it could come from a greater entity. You've perhaps heard of stories, typically old legends, where gods and deities have come to earth to speak to disciples and to pass on messages and actions. Although we're talking about occurrences from a universal standpoint, these are similar events. There's little doubt the two are connected.

I was very close to my grandma since I was a child, but she grew ill quite violently and unfortunately passed away. I spent many years tormenting myself with what could have been different. If only I had worked harder so I could afford better healthcare or could have given her a better life.

In my late twenties, there came a time when my mother started to fall ill, and I tortured myself even more. I wasn't in a position to do things differently, and it was as though history was repeating itself, which of course, bought up all those old feelings, and I found myself in a bit of an emotional rut.

It wasn't until one night when I was feeling particularly overwhelmed that I decided to go for a walk. I was walking around the block, and since I lived in New York City, the streets were still reasonably buzzing with activity. I sat at one of the bus stops and tried to take my mind off things by watching the world go past.

I didn't even realize the elderly gentleman who came to sit next to me. Lost in my own head, it didn't occur to me until a few days later that a man of his age would not be out at this time of night, nor would he be wearing the extremely fancy clothes he had on. He seemed dressed for a suit and tie event, but a very dated one, like in the 60s.

He sat down and broke the ice with small talk, talking about the evening and the crowds, and asked if I was okay because I seemed down. I briefly explained my situation, how I was overwhelmed with feelings about my late grandmother, and how I felt as though I let her down or could have done better.

A silence hung in the air for a minute or two before he replied.

> "My child. Evelyn knew you did your best, and she loves that you put the effort you did, but things couldn't have gone any other way. She knows that everything happened exactly as they were meant to. She's just grateful that you were able to prove just how much you loved her. She loves you. And all she wants from you is to fondly look back at the good times you were able to share. She wants you to forgive yourself."

I listened while staring at the pavement and let his words sink in. Something in how he said each sentence made them stand out and really struck something within me. It was profound. Random, of course, but so pure. I didn't just hear what he was saying. I felt it. I was fully grounded and in the moment.

Before responding, I looked up, broke my reverie, turned to look at him, and found he was gone. The street was practically empty, and the elderly man was nowhere to be seen. A profound experience for sure, and one that stuck with me for years.

However, while I knew of the existence of spirit guides and guardian angels, it wasn't until a tarot reading several years later that the psychic described the entire event practically word for word that I realized that I had experienced my own introduction.

From then on, I have mostly kept my eyes open for new signs from my spirit guides, and tried to learn more and more about them, how and why they appear to us, and what we can do to open ourselves up to more experiences from them. Here is what I've discovered.

An Introduction to Spirit Guides

Many people use different terms for different ways the universe tries to contact us, but realistically, they all fall under the term spirit guides. Even guardian angels are technically spirit guides. There are six main types of spirit guides you'll want to keep your eyes open for, and we'll be diving into this throughout the chapter.

These spirit guides can appear to you at any time, or they could be with you always. Some guides will be new, and others having existed long before you were even born. Others will come and go as and when you need them. You can even use your internal free will and consciousness to manifest the appearance of a spirit guide when you need one.

Spirit guides tend to fall under one or more of these six categories:

Archangels

Archangels are a type of angel that act as leaders to other angels. They have a tremendous amount of energy within them and are magnificently powerful. If you're an empathic kind of person (an empath), you will feel a shift in the energy or mood when an archangel enters the room. The atmosphere will change.

Archangels are limited in their forms, and there are specific archangels for specific reasons. For example, the Archangel Raphael is known as the Archangel of Healing and can work with an infinite number of human beings at any time and in many ways, both big and small.

There are between seven and 15 archangels, depending on your source and how deep you want to go into the topic. The 15 archangels are:

- Ariel

- Azrael

- Chamuel

- Gabriel

- Haniel

- Jeremiel

- Jophiel

- Metatron

- Michael

- Raguel

- Raphael

- Raziel

- Sandalphone

- Uriel

- Zadkiel

Ascended Masters

Ascended Masters are high-profile spirit guides. They are beings who were once human but transcended because they lived incredibly spiritual lives. They include beings like Buddha and the Virgin Mother Mary. They are beings who are regarded as powerful spiritual leaders.

Legends and assumed knowledge are that all ascended masters are spirit guides who work together in peace regardless of religion or culture, to carry the universe's messages to those who need to hear them.

Departed Loved Ones

Perhaps one of the most common forms of spirit guides because they're more personal to us individually and likelier to be recognized. These spirit guides choose whether they want to provide guidance as and when they please, and may be people you knew throughout your living life or ancestors from previous generations.

In essence, any human being, not even a loved one or someone you knew, could be become your spirit guide. For example, if you're a musician, you may find other musician spirit guides contacting you and offering guidance when the time is right because you're connected to them through your art, which puts you at the same vibrational frequency.

Guardian Angels

Guardian angels are special. They are angelic spirit guides who guide only you. You do not share them and you can have more than one. Guardian angels are spiritual beings, vibrational forces, or form of universal energy that have devoted their existence to help you.

This is a mission that could traverse light and time, and they can be called upon for assistance whenever you need them. They are energetic beings who love you unconditionally, forever and always. Through all the good and the bad.

Helper Angels

Helper angels could easily be described as 'freelance angels.' They are angels who help living beings and the flow of cosmic energy and messaging of their own accord. They find individuals to assist and will summon themselves, or can be summoned, to specific situations they can help with.

Helper angels typically appear during lighter moments, perhaps during a dream to give you a sense of direction, during meditation, or in a fleeting thought or idea.

Spirit Animals

Spirit animals are fascinating. They commonly appear in the form of a pet you once had. This is usually the case because humans and pets tend to have incredibly strong emotional and physical bonds. They depend on each other both for peace of mind and physical survival

However, spirit animals can appear in any form they like, or if you're summoning them, in any form you want. Most people have a spirit animal that resonates with only them. My spirit animal is a wolf, and whenever I need some guidance or I'm looking for signs from the universe, they usually manifest themselves in the form of a wolf.

Summoning your spirit animal can be as simple as connecting with imagery or feelings of your favorite animal. Spirit animals can show up anywhere at any time, as an idea, on television, in your backyard, in the street, printed on a t-shirt, or in conversation, so need to keep your eyes peeled.

With that, we've come to the end of the third chapter. You now know the most common spirit guides and ways the universe can contact you. From this point, think about looking for these spirit guides in your own life.

They may come to you naturally, you may have memories of them appearing to you, or you may wish to summon them consciously. We'll explore this in the next chapter.

CHAPTER FOUR

Making First Contact

"Please don't worry. I've got you."
– the universe

I've been contacted by spirit guides and heard the universe's call several times throughout my life. Initially, I was inexperienced and didn't know what I was looking for or what was going on, and I only accepted this acknowledgment in hindsight. Sometimes, this was days after the event or even years.

However, with greater understanding of what spirit guides are, what the call sounds like, and how this kind of messaging and experience works, I became a lot more present with my experiences, not only recognizing when they happened but actively making them happen.

Within the pages of this chapter is how to make first contact with the universe, in whatever way you want to connect with them. We're going to dive into some of the techniques you can use, how you can open your heart and soul to this, and how you can reconnect with the universe in the most powerful ways.

Conversations with the Universe

It is possible to have a conversation with the universe. When the great cosmos is sending you signs and trying to show you something to help you decide or give you a new perspective on some issues, this is first contact.

This is the universe saying, 'hey, this is something you need to look at and a new idea for you to consider.' In some cases, this may be all you need. In my friend's experience, she was in a very toxic relationship, and all the signs clearly showed her how to get help to get out. In your own experiences, the signs may not be enough.

Its times like when you see a sign and you want to dive deeper. These situations happen all the time. The universe is always speaking to you, but some signs will be more important than others, and some you won't care to think about. There's nothing wrong with this since you can't physically take every opportunity that comes your way.

Regardless, how do you converse with the universe? It can sound so far-fetched, even more so the more you think about it, but let's take a deep breath and start at the beginning.

First, get clear.

You need to have a clear idea of what you want to talk about before moving forward with your conversation. If you go into the conversation umming and ahhing, you're probably not going to get anywhere, and you're certainly not going to leave with a clear answer. The worst thing you can do is leave more confused than when you started.

Slow down and get clarity. What are you asking for? What do you want? Do you want to know how to approach your career? Your relationships? Your financial situation? How to clear your mind and find peace? Are you stressed, anxious, or depressed and not sure what to do about it?

One of the best tips I ever learned, specifically when it comes to reading tarot cards (which is another way you can communicate with the universe), is to ask a specific questions that don't have yes or no answers. For example:

- What can I focus on to be more creative tomorrow?

- What are some of the ways I can be happier in my relationship?

- What can I do to make today's day at work great?

- How can I approach a new person in my life?

- What can I focus on to make my life more fulfilling and satisfying?

These questions are ideal because you can receive actionable answers and ideas that can help you get a sense of direction, no matter what area of your life you're working on. If it helps, write down what you want to talk about beforehand. Remember, especially when starting out, that you might need to repeat this process daily until you can receive a clear answer.

Once you're clear on what you want to talk about, it's time to open your mind to the possibilities and the greater power source. Find a quiet space, somewhere you feel comfortable, and sit quietly. Try to ground yourself in the present moment and clearly ask what you want.

Say something like, "I am here to ask you about how I can be happier in my relationships and what I can do. I am unfortunate right now and am looking for answers."

Repeat this statement in your mind. At first, you will get a lot of background ego chatter, which we have developed over the years. Call it anxiety, stress, worry, or whatever you want, it's hard to overcome.

You'll probably find your mind wandering and new thoughts distracting you. Thoughts like what you're having for dinner, what emails you've got to deal with, what you're up to during the weekend, how you're going to deal with a personal situation, etc. It takes time and patience (and a massive amount of forgiveness and compassion towards yourself) to overcome and be able to see through these ways of thinking.

You will experience good days and bad days. Some days the call of the universe will be murky and almost like a whisper, and other days it will be crystal clear. Accept what is and listen. Some days you can subject yourself to a very intense and profound experience, and some days will be quiet and almost as though you're hearing nothing. Both are acceptable. Trust the process.

With this understanding, you can truly begin. Ask your question and listen for the replies that come your way. What messages appear in your mind? I remember having some very intense experiences.

One time, I was feeling very lost, and my life felt like a mess. My career was up in the air and uncertain, my relationship was intense, and everything seemed to stress me out.

I knelt on my bedroom floor, eyes closed, hands resting on my legs with my palms facing the sky and asked the universe for help.

Intensely, it was as though I felt the fingertips of a woman slowly making their way up my arms. Her touch was gentle and soft, and while intense and incredibly profound at first, I kept my eyes closed and allowed the experience to happen. Her fingertips traveled down my arms, across my palms, and eventually closed my hands into fists, her hands resting on top.

Feeling the manifestation of a woman in the space in front of me, I felt a breeze across my skin, and in that same air, there was a whisper. It spoke to me.

"Everything is going to be okay. Breathe deep. Give it time."

That's exactly what I needed to hear. In my stressed out, overwhelmed, and anxious state, I just needed someone to remind me that I needed to give things time to resolve. I needed patience, and I needed to try and calm down, not falling into the perpetual trap of stressed-out thinking cycles.

I took a deep breath and opened my eyes. Everything seemed brighter and more vivid. My relentless mind seemed to have calmed, and I continued with the rest of my day and week with a refreshed, calm, and focused mindset. The universe had spoken to me, and through its words, I had been freed from my old ways of thinking and set onto a new chapter.

Be open to the tiny signals, whispers, signs, and messages that the universe is sending you, whether you're sitting down for a quiet conversation or in your day-to-day life. Pay attention to the details.

Listen to your feelings. If you feel an urge or an intense spark of emotion, this is a sign you need to focus on. If you think about a topic and you feel tension in your body, this could be a sign. For example, if you ask whether a new career opportunity is right for you and you feel a painful sensation or discomfort, this is clearly a no. If you feel happy, excited, and peaceful, then you can take this as a yes.

Remember, there's no limit to how many questions you can ask or how many times you can contact the universe. The more you do it, the better you'll be at connecting and listening to the answer. However, it's important to remember that conversing with the universe does not solve your problems, nor does it count as action.

The universe exists to guide you and to help open your mind, but it's still up to you to act and make decisions. If you listen to an answer but keep living your life the way you do now, nothing will change and you'll have effectively ignored your call.

Contacting Your Spirit Guides

In addition to speaking to the universe, you can also seek guidance from your spirit guides and all the various forms they come in. There are many ways you can do this, the most common of which I'll dive into now.

Just like the universe communicates with you, your spirit guides can first contact you by sending you signs such as synchronicities or other forms of meaningful coincidences, which makes sense since both the universe and your spirit guides come from the same source of power,. For example, you may see a number repeatedly in your life, or you hear a song on the radio that resonates with the day you've just had.

Keep your eyes open for these impactful and notable situations that stand out from the monotony of everyday life. You may experience a dream that stands out to you with a specific message, or you may even have your guide appear to you within the dream itself.

Spirit guides also work in the background of your life and may not approach you directly. For example, they may guide another person into your life who asks you out for lunch or calls, or they may encourage certain events to happen. To improve your chances of catching these signs and connecting with these messages, practice the following:

- Become more present in your day-to-day life through increased awareness, meditation, journaling practices, etc.

- Take a minute or two each day to look out for signs from your spirit guides whenever you do something or change your scenery.

- Set time aside to allow natural connections from your spirit guides on a daily, weekly, or monthly basis and on special events, such as the night of the full moon or a new year

- Practice simplifying the messages of what you're asking for or on the topics you want to know

- Use a tool to help, whether it's a human psychic to help encourage a connection to your spirit guides or a divination tool.

Of course, you don't need to wait for your spirit guides to show you a sign but instead can reach out to them as and when you need them. Just like with asking the universe for guidance, you're first going to need to be clear with exactly what you want from your conversation. Otherwise, the replies you get will be murky and difficult to understand.

Once you're clear on what you want (repeating the process I spoke about in the previous section of this chapter), you'll want to sit in a quiet space, away from distraction, where you'll be able to connect with a guide of your choice peacefully. You can specifically ask for the guidance of a specific guide (check the list in the previous chapter), or you can address the universe and see which guides appear to you.

Sit quietly and peacefully and zone into your thoughts and the sensations of your mind and body. See what you feel and acknowledge what thoughts come to mind but try not to get lost in the thought itself. Just acknowledge and become mindful of the topic, and then move on. Just flow with your thoughts.

Once you start reaching a sound state of mind, perhaps after a few minutes, repeat the question you want to ask in your mind. Repeat it, focusing on the message and what you're trying to achieve, attempting to be as clear as possible with what you want. Then, wait for an answer.

This can take some time, or it may happen instantly. Use this opportunity when you first feel something to start to get to know your spirit guides. After all, you're with your spirit guides for life, so you can benefit greatly from getting to know them. When you're starting out, it's important to open your mind to possible names or identities.

See what names come instinctively to mind, and if none do, you can name them yourself. There are plenty of spirit guides who are open to this and will, in fact, encourage it because you'll have a much more personal connection with them.

Again, the more you practice, the better you'll become, and soon you'll have a whole list of spirit guides that you can connect with. Remember, some may appear once, while others could appear seemingly all the time. The best way to track this is to keep a spirit guide journal, which is basically a diary where you'll jot down your experiences, helping you to remember who you've connected with and your journey so far.

It's by repeating this process that you'll deepen your connections. You can meditate with your spirit guides as much or as little as you like, but if you're starting out, then try practicing at least once a week, perhaps to prepare yourself for the start of your upcoming week, to help you become familiar with who your spirit guides are and how to connect with them.

Practice just sending your messages and your questions with your thoughts, but don't be afraid to branch out. There are other tools you can use for your spirit guides to channel their messages through. Tools like tarot cards, chance encounters, oracle cards, and runes provide the opportunity for your spirit guides to get in touch.

If you want to try this out for yourself right now, place your hands in front of you and hold something of meaning. For example, to contact a departed loved one, hold one of their possessions, or their photograph. You could hold a crystal, a bible, a tarot card you feel drawn to, or anything along these lines. It can be whatever you like, or more importantly, whatever object or thing your instinct guides you to.

Hold this item for a minute, cycle some deep breaths, and close your eyes, continuing to mindfully breathe to center yourself, and ask your spirit guides to reveal themselves or send you a message via the item you're holding. See the effects for yourself, tuning into both the item and your thoughts and feelings for an answer.

Harnessing the Power of Angel Numbers

We've already touched on angel numbers, but while it seems like I've focused on a lot of other aspects of connecting with your universe, your guides, and hearing the calls, you now know everything you need to know to fully harness the power of angel numbers in all aspects of your life.

Let's explore an example. Let's say you wake up at 3:20 am. You shrug it off and go back to bed. You wake up and go to work and catch the 320 bus or see a car you're stuck behind in traffic with 320 on the registration plate. You get a coffee from the local cafe, and your bill comes to $3.20. You get to work, and there are 320 new workflow updates, and so on.

The repetition of the number 320 is a message from the universe and your spirit angels, and you're only letting yourself down if you choose to ignore it. Fortunately, this is not a new or unknown concept. All you need to do is look up your angel number online or use an angel number book to see what the meaning is.

In this case, 320 refers to the connection of the individual numbers 3, 2, and 0. 3 represents encouragement and support, communication, and self-expression. It's a number that refers to creating or manifesting something. 2 is about harmony and balance. It's about having trust and faith in what you're doing and following the path to fulfilling your life's purpose.

0 is the number of balance and Zen. It's the 'God Force' number and encompasses wholeness, completion, universal energies, and everything becoming one. Whenever this number appears, you should amplify the complete meaning to universal proportions and levels of importance.

Overall, the number 320 means that you have a strong connection to the universe's guides and messaging, and that this connection is key to following what you want to achieve in your life, whatever it is you're focusing on, be it your relationships, career, personal life, and so on.

However, there is a very strong focus on creativity. Whether you want peace, happiness, joy, satisfaction, or results, this number signifies that you should have faith and trust in your creative abilities. No matter what area of your life you're focusing on, it's time to communicate openly with what you're doing and let those creative juices flow.

It means staying positive and hopeful in terms of what the future holds and taking the plunge. You have the skills, knowledge, and talent to achieve the outcome what you want. It's time to engage and make that happen.

Angel numbers can be any number, usually up to three digits long, but they can be any length, and they work alongside the principles of numerology. To notice these numbers is a sign you're on the right path, but it's also a sign to get in touch with the universe. If you can, you'll be able to identify a sense of direction regarding how you can move forward in your given situation.

The Moments of Disconnect

With time and practice, as you start to experience connections with your spirit guides and the universe itself, there will also be harder times when you experience a disconnect. You may experience moments where you're trying to connect with your spirit guides and you feel like you're doing everything right, but you can't seem to hear a message.

I went through this quite recently. It was as though the universe fell quiet. There were whispers in the ether, but there was no clear communication, especially compared to the clear and sometimes quite intense conversations I had been having up to that point.

It was scary, and to be honest, I felt alone. I almost felt abandoned. Imagine the thoughts crossing your mind when you feel like the universe has abandoned you. It's not a pleasant place to be, and it will not last forever.

First, and most importantly, your spirit guides will never abandon you or leave you alone. They will always be by your side. Next, remember your spirit guides can also be working in the background of your life and may not approach you directly. If you feel a disconnect in your life, it may be a sign to become more present, ultimately opening yourself up to any chances of inspiration that may come your way.

This may typically happen during the most difficult and most challenging times of your life, which is why it can feel so scary and abrupt. However, take this as a reminder that your spirit guides want to be as close to you as they can.

Therefore, take special care to connect with your spirit guides, even more so than usual. This could be through journaling or through a meditation practice that you engage in. If you do so for ten minutes a day, try 20 minutes. If you meditate weekly, try daily. If you don't use tarot cards or divination tools, you may want to try them.

If you put a little more effort into connecting with your spiritual guides, stating clearly that you need their attention, then they will listen, and they will respond. It's just a matter of time and opening up to them. Sometimes, you just need to take that little extra step.

Looking to the Future

You should have everything you need to open your mind, your soul, and the real you to the calls from the universe and your spirit guides and the messages and connections they have for you. On a tangent, your spirit guides have always been by your side, and the universe has always been communicating with you. You've probably experienced these situations before, you now know what to look for and how to embrace it.

Looking into the future, in addition to learning new, perhaps more advanced, ways of connecting, you just need to practice. Think of when you were a child, and everything was new. Your connection to the universe was at its greatest because your mind was fresh, and the signs were everywhere.

However, as you grow older, your mind becomes conditioned to think in certain ways, and you start to lose connection with the universal powers that be. Instead, the mind begins to focus on other things, such as chasing happiness, money, relationships, and just trying to cope and comprehend the growing complexities of the modern world, a lot of which were created by those who lost their connections and do not seek to reconnect.

Nevertheless, with practice, perseverance, and an open mind, you can start to relax some of the more conditioned ways of thinking that you've developed over the years and reconnect with the cosmic source that is. And once you're there, the world becomes your oyster, and your life really does become your life.

Conclusion

And with that, we've come to the end of our journey. Hopefully, you found this book a little inspiring, and I hope that I managed to help you understand some of the experiences you've already gone through in your life, as well as helping you set up for even greater and more insightful experiences that can happen in your future.

Again, this book is only meant to serve as a detailed beginner guide. While short and sweet, there's more than enough information to get you started on your journey and to help you connect to the universe in a way that can really benefit your life. But don't think this is the be-all and end-all.

There's a world of wonder, mystery, and magic out there, forces of power and nature that we can't even begin to comprehend. Simply ask yourself questions like what happens at the edge of the universe, what's beyond it, and how it all began, and you should start to glimmer what potential there is.

I highly recommend that you start small and apply these concepts to your own life. Be as confident as you can be and open your mind to the potential and see the proof unfold. I wish you the best of luck on your journey, and I'm excited to hear from you.

If you found any kind of insight from this book, you enjoyed reading it, learned something, found it helpful, or just want to connect, be sure to leave a review on the page where you purchased this book. I'm very excited to hear your thoughts, and through your feedback, I can journey on to become the best writer I can be, a path laid out for me by my own instinct and guided along by my own spirit guides.

Until next time, good luck, and may the universe be forever on your side.

Book #2

Hoodoo Book of Spells for Beginners

Easy and effective Rootwork, Conjuring, and Protection Spells for Healing and Prosperity

Introduction

It was during the hardest times that I discovered Hoodoo, and the power that this sorcery holds.

I've dabbled with various spiritual practices throughout my life, but few of them have stuck with me in the way Hoodoo has. Originating within the African American populations, mainly in the southern United States, Hoodoo magic is a relatively new form of magic on the grand scale of time, but its impact has changed the lives of endless people across the world indefinitely.

While not as popular today as it once was, Hoodoo magic still plays a big part in the lives of those who practice it - practitioners known as rootworkers or root doctors, but don't let this mislead you. Hoodoo is so much more than the chemistry and alchemy of roots, herbs, and spices, as you'll discover throughout this book.

My Personal Experience Awakened

I've personally been familiar with Hoodoo from a young age. While my parents were Jehovah's Witnesses, it was always Hoodoo magic that held a special place in my heart. Magic that interested me in a way I couldn't quite describe.

My grandmother was someone who swore by it. I remember sitting and watching her create potions in her home, going out and collecting ingredients wherever she could, and playing with some of the more elaborately designed bottles and potion vials she had collected over the years.

But still, I struggled to grasp Hoodoo myself. Although I was introduced all those years ago, I had yet to give myself to the practice and open myself up. In hindsight, I now understand it was simply that the time wasn't right. In fact, that time didn't come until around a decade ago when I was sitting in my apartment during some of my darker days. My emotions stewed inside me despite all my tears having already flowed.

I had found myself in a bad relationship. An explosively violent one. I now see my ex-partner living with his own demons, and while I'm still sure we loved each other in our own way, we weren't meant to be. Regardless, it was during one of the more intense fights I truly started to realize this for perhaps the first time. He had left our apartment and went to stay with a friend. I was left alone in my own space, hunched over at the kitchen table in the darkness, the only light coming from the streetlight on the other side of the street.

I was lost, confused, and entirely unsure of what my future held. It was at this moment, literally sitting with my head in my hands, that the shimmers of Hoodoo began to draw my attention gently. At first, I was taken a little by surprise, but this was soon replaced by feelings of intrigue and curiosity. All the little pieces of information I had discovered over the years slowly started to piece themselves together inside my mind in a way they had not done before. The curiosity seemed to consume me.

I pulled out a book my grandmother had passed down to me many years before from the bookcase and flicked through the pages for an hour or so, not really sure what I was looking for. Eventually, about midway through, I came across a recipe for a potion of happiness. I laughed to myself. Could it really be that simple?

I thought back to my grandmother all those years ago. I had so much love and respect for that lady in my life, so hey, if she was adamant it worked, then maybe I should be too. It took a while and a strange walk outside in the middle of the night to the Bronx park, but I managed to collect all the ingredients.

I searched the apartment for bits and pieces I could use. The book was old, torn at the spine with several missing pages, but most were present. It was a book of protection spells and described roots, herbs, spices,

A little under an hour later, the potion was set, and I recited the spell written among the pages. I also spent a few minutes writing down any intentions I had onto small scraps of paper, folding them up and tying them to the potion vial, and sat with the setup for half an hour or so and meditating on my intentions.

At first, I thought I wanted freedom from my suffering, and there's no doubt I did. My sadness was almost overwhelming, and I just wanted it to end. This was my main intention, but this quickly faded to the back of my mind, and without warning, made way for something a little more profound.

I felt peaceful. I felt calm, but I also felt determined. There was a moment, a lasting moment in the stillness, that seemed to stretch on and on where I felt determined. I felt motivated. I felt driven. I knew I was in a rut, but I would feel a burning drive within me that knew that if I put my mind to it, I would be able to move forward.

At the time, I thought it was simply a moment of realization. An epiphany, and perhaps to some degree it was. However, I know now, coupled with my more recent experiences over the years, that this was some kind of magic. Ever since, time and time again, I've been able to tap into this source of power that's not just within me but a kind of magic that's within us all.

What is Hoodoo Magic?

At its core, by dictionary definition, Hoodoo is an art form used to conjure, manifest, and exchange physical and spiritual powers. A magic used to generate and attract wealth, good health, increased fortunes, and to improve relationships. A magic used to help you define your intentions and to give you a sense of direction that enables you to overcome and conquer any challenges or obstacles you may face at any point in your life.

It's a set of spiritual practices, traditions, and beliefs with origins rooted in the Black African communities that North America and Europeans wrongfully enslaved over the last 300 years. A way for human beings to allow supernatural forces into their lives in an attempt to improve them.

The word 'Hoodoo' first appeared in written documents around 1870, but the true origins are unknown. As you may have guessed from the spelling, the word is believed to have originated from the word 'Voodoo,' although the two practices are quite different, as will be explained later in this chapter.

As painful as it is to conceptualize, over 12 million people were enslaved and transported from the African continent to North America (what is now the United States) between the 16th and 19th Centuries, a truly traumatic experience, the effects and consequences of which still ripple out around the world through people like us to this day.

It was within these enslaved, African, becoming African-American communities, the art of Hoodoo found its feet, rooting itself in the culture to eventually blossom into what it is today.

However, a form of Hoodoo was already practiced in Africa, but here it was regarded as a religion, but soon became regarded as a way of magic. Allow me to bring some perspective to this.

If you lived in 18th Century American as a Black slave, you did not share the same medical care as those living in the European-American communities. Black communities, therefore, needed to create their own support and healthcare systems and their own ways of looking after themselves, both for the enslaved and free. This includes psychological care, emotional and spiritual support, and so on.

Black communities had no choice but to rely on the knowledge and spirit of the people around them, those who were also suffering. With nowhere to go and no one to turn to, they had only the love, support, and knowledge of each other. It was within this practice of care, communication, and the coming togetherness that allowed those in suffering to process their trauma and find some kind of healing from the tragic situations they found themselves in.

Since enslaved people were taken from all over the African continent, they came from various cultures, societies, and ethnic backgrounds. With such diversity coming together in one place, Hoodoo was a way of bringing these people together in a union of respect and compassion. Hoodoo is, therefore, almost a cocktail of magic, love, respect, and community from all these various places that would otherwise have not come together. I believe that that, in a beautiful way, is a kind of magic in itself.

This means modern Hoodoo is a mixture of religion and magical practices that have all come together under severely intense circumstances, making it one of the most powerful forces there is.

There's no doubt the significant influences of Hoodoo come from the Central African regions. Evidence suggests around 40% of all enslaved Africans came from these central regions, specifically the Bantu-Kongo areas. This is evident within Hoodoo practices since there are clear links to the Kongo cosmogram and Kongolese beliefs and practices.

The other significant influence comes from the Western African region, introducing various components, such as the magical mojo bag. Many of the ships traveling to and from North America landed on the West African coast, from where the slave trade was managed and organized. It should come as no surprise that there were sadly many people enslaved from this area. There is also clear evidence of magical influence from West African Muslim communities, whose members resided in these areas during slave trading periods.

Nowadays, Hoodoo is practiced within the more subtle veins of society. Its practitioners are often called 'root workers' or 'root doctors' since they emphasize working with herbs, roots, and plants. Although it's most often referred to as 'root working,' in general, it's important to remember that this is just one aspect of Hoodoo practice.

Interestingly, what sets Hoodoo apart from other forms of Western or European magic, and what makes it appealing to many, is that there's no need to practice any kind of summoning, nor do you need to negotiate or form relationships with other spirits, forms, or entities. While the 19th Century brought about a lot of Christian influence in the practice, Hoodoo practitioners do believe in a God of sorts, but there's not a significant emphasis on the God themselves.

The Hoodoo God is a genderless entity, but they are neither good nor evil, despite very strong ideas on what good and evil are within Hoodoo practices. God is the supreme being responsible for the creation of the world, but this God is not concerned with the goings-on of humankind. There are lesser entities and spirits that are involved in these activities.

The Boo Hag is one such spirit. An umbrella term, a Boo Hag is a spirit that exists to torment and scare living people. They have magical, spiritual powers that can kill or cure people of diseases, predict the future, or help people find things.

When you consider where Hoodoo magic came from, you should see why this makes sense. For example, populations of African Americans in Indiana refused to enter a certain location because it was 'haunted by the spirits of the Black people who were beaten to death.' This is the work of the Boo Hag.

But not all spirits are evil or come from a place of pain, misfortune, and torment. There are spirits that protect from pain and suffering, spirits that bring peace and calm to intense situations or settle intense feelings, and spirits that reside within the elements, such as the MIA, the West African water spirit.

However, while I could write an entire book on the history and the spiritual world of Hoodoo, the most important thing to remember about the history is the fact that it was born out of suffering and is a practice deeply rooted in the hearts and the lives of your ancestors.

This is where the magic gets its power.

The Links Between Voodoo and Hoodoo

Hoodoo magic is not Voodoo magic, and there are some core similarities and differences you may want to help better your understanding of what this practice is actually all about.

This is the first distinction you need to make. There are similarities, but the two are not the same, but they are certainly related. In mainstream culture, Hoodoo is very much used to describe any form of native American or African culture magic. Voodoo is a religion, also known as a magical tradition. Both have elements of African and European influence.

However, Hoodoo has loose ties with Catholic Christianity, whereas Voodoo has ties with Protestant Christianity. Don't mistake that practitioners have to be Christian following in any sense.

Voodoo magic is very much its own religious practice, one that stems from countries like Haiti, with some ties to West African populations. Within Voodoo, you must walk the path that gets you ordained in the religion, and there must be leaders present to oversee the magic performed. There are also numerous deities, gods, entities, and spirits that must be worshiped and respected for the practices to be followed correctly.

None of these requirements are necessary, nor exist, within Hoodoo practices. Practitioners don't need to believe or follow any gods, and you're free to worship any other Gods or deities you may respect or believe in. There's no ruling hierarchy to follow, such as having overseers, priests, or other ordained individuals who would theoretically be 'higher up' than you.

Hoodoo has no strict structure that needs to be followed like in other religions. Hoodoo is a practice that you find and connect with within yourself for your own benefit. You're not trying to serve some greater purpose or worship an entity. That's why Hoodoo can be best described as personal magic.

In the modern world, the terms Hoodoo and Voodoo are very much used interchangeably, even though this is wrong. It's simply a misconception by those who don't know any better. In reality, modern Hoodoo, especially 'non-African' Hoodoo, seems to borrow some aspects of Voodoo magic but is more seen by those who practice it as a more Christianized variation of the well-established and more dominantly practiced Voodoo that is practiced in countries like Haiti.

Remember, despite the popular opinion that the mainstream public seems to hold on Voodoo being used for evil purposes, this is just not the case. Hoodoo seems to fall under this category for a lot of people for the same reasons, but the opposite is right. Both Voodoo and Hoodoo can be used for good, for healing, and for prosperity, but there can be more malicious practices, should that be what the user intends to use the magic for, as there can be for any substance of practice in this world.

To cut a long story short, Hoodoo is not Voodoo. There are certainly similarities, but they are not the same. There are many varieties of each, and for this book, we're going to be focusing mainly on Black Hoodoo, or the Hoodoo created by the African American communities. Interestingly, this is a magic that stems from African Voodoo, but with European influence, since it was created when Europeans took slaves to America, and the two cultures intertwined, hence the Christian influences.

As you'll see later on, this is why many of Hoodoo spells use recitals from the psalms and bible passages, and there are many ties to Christian passages.

There is also a stem of Hoodoo known as 'White Hoodoo,' but this is the term given to practitioners who don't have African origins. These are still non-white people, but they weren't enslaved by other Africans, nor come from African descent.

Due to the history of Hoodoo, it's a magic only Black people can practice.

CHAPTER ONE

Hoodoo in the Modern World

"In hoodooism, anything that you do is the plan of God, understand? God has something to do with everything that you do whether it's good or bad, he's got something to do with it... You'll get what's coming to you."
- Translated practitioner

In today's modern world, there are issues and difficulties I've experienced, and there's no doubt these problems have affected you in some way at some point in your life. Aspects of your life like money, relationships, landlords, careers, health, and everything else that affects you, both big and small.

One thing you can be sure of in life is that it's going to throw curveballs and challenges your way. You need to figure out how to deal with these situations for the sake of your own health, wellbeing, and inner peace.

Hoodoo is a methodology, a process, and an art form that can help you to find the answers you're looking for. It's a spiritual practice to help you reconnect with yourself at your core, not just with who you are as an individual, but also with your history. Your ancestry. Your past.

Hoodoo acts as a light to illuminate your way during the darker times. It holds back and protects you from shadows that may be lurking on the horizon, just out of sight.

My experience with Hoodoo has been one of progression and salvation, the results of which have encouraged me to write about them in the hopes that you can feel inspired enough to open your heart and your mind to the wonders of Hoodoo.

It's not an easy task. Hoodoo's history is long and stems from a dark place. A place of pain and suffering, but that's one part of life that will never change. Instead, it's time to make peace with this discomfort by embracing it and overcoming it. It may sound a little scary, but this book exists to guide you to a place where this is possible.

You've come so far already, and by holding this book in your hands right now, it's a sign you're ready to take the next step. I know, deep down in my very essence, that you're seeking the same thing that I once did, and now you're on the cusp of discovery.

You seek answers. You crave a path to walk. You're determined to discover clarity. There's a spark inside you, burning for you to reconnect with yourself, your instinct, and your inner and spiritual being. It's time to learn how to trust yourself and your inner knowledge, unlocking your full potential in any situation. It's time to manifest your desires, your wants, and to start living the life you want.

To some, this may seem like an impossible idea, but it isn't.

Never before has an intentional art such as Hoodoo been more important or so potentially valuable in the lives of so many people. Becoming familiar with such an art can unlock so many doors within your life while helping you move past the potential obstacles that hold you back.

Throughout the following chapters, we're going to explore the ins and outs of Hoodoo ideas, sharing the knowledge that has been passed down for generations.

I'm going to dive into the history of Hoodoo, where it came from, and what stories make up this practice's origins. We'll explore the rules and guidelines and how you can start to master the process and use it in your day-to-day life.

This book will serve as a beginner's guide. An introduction. A nudge in the right direction provides enough information to get you started and stand firmly on your own two feet.

This isn't about some long-lost magic or practice that creates wondrous effects as you see in movies. This is about intention.

This is about connecting your mind with your spirit and your soul. It's about healing and processing traumas and protecting yourself from any dangers you may encounter in the future. It's about finding peace during the hardest times so you can shine brightly once again.

If, for the last few years, and perhaps many years of your life, you have been stricken with darkness and troubles, by turning these pages, you allow yourself the opportunity to light a candle to find your way.

And with that, set the spark that sets this journey off in the best possible way. The candle is lit.

Turn the page and go forth.

How to Use Hoodoo in the Modern World

Hoodoo was born out of a need. It stemmed from the pain and suffering of Black people. Therefore, it's a magic that only Black people can practice. In the past, it would have been used for all kinds of purposes, including:

- Promoting happiness within families and communities

- Increasing fortunes and chances of favorable situations

- Reducing feelings of pain and suffering

- Healing traumas and both physical and emotional hurt

- Nurturing protection again future dangers

- Exacting revenge on those who cause pain

These are clearly situations that haunt many of us today, and you've perhaps experienced them already. Times are turbulent, and perhaps to an extent they always will be, which is why Hoodoo will remain relevant.

If you want to practice Hoodoo and you want to experience this magic in your life, you need to be able to connect to its history and its origins on a deeper level and relate this pain, suffering, and togetherness to your own. Yes, it can be painful, and it hurts. Yes, it can be traumatic, and there are places, certainly in your own past, that you may not want to go to, but you need to open your mind to the call of your ancestors to channel their energy.

We'll take things step by step, but remind yourself that there is no need to be scared. Or afraid. This is a path many have walked, and many will walk after you. Open your soul, and let's walk together.

And it's on that note that you should now be ready to take your first steps into the world of Hoodoo. It's time to reconnect with this magical practice and see the benefits for yourself.

Take a deep breath as you reconnect with this historical power, turn to your new chapter, and let's begin.

CHAPTER TWO

Getting Started with Rootwork/Hoodoo

"The psychic witch lives in a state of enchantment, seeing all things as magickal and understanding that the universe is composed of endless possibilities and potential. The psychic witch sees a door where others see a wall."
— **Mat Auryn**

When I first started to connect with my magical core, I felt a mix of emotions. I was excited and curious about what was going to happen, but I would be lying if I didn't say I was a little scared. After all, what was going to happen? What happened if I accidentally connected with some profound dark energy or spirit, some entity of trauma and suffering that I couldn't escape?

These fears certainly crossed my mind, but I knew that my intention was clear and pure deep down in my heart. I wanted to find peace, and I wanted to discover a light that could lead me through my own darkness. Since my own personal journey began during some of the darker times of my life, I wanted to push through my insecurities to find out more.

But it's important to remember you don't need to walk alone. There are many people on the same path as you, people starting out and those who will start out, and I, too, was once in your position. There is also the entirety of your ancestors behind you, the people from whom you came from; many of whom would have been involved with their own Hoodoo practices and may have even been there at its origin.

When getting started with Hoodoo practices, you first need to open your mind to this realization. You need to do the same with your soul and your heart. Open yourself to the magical guidance that lies before you. If you want to be elevated through the magic, you need to let it in, and while this notion may seem easy, it's a tricky thing to do and not something that will happen overnight.

Unfortunately, opening your mind is not something that can be strictly taught but is instead a process of crossing the obstacles in your way as you discover them. Opportunities will come and go, such as if you're having a particularly stressful time. It's when you become mindful that this stressful or painful time is, in fact, an opportunity to connect to Hoodoo magic that you'll start to see what it's capable of. It starts with mindfulness.

For example, if you find your relationship is on the rocks and you're experiencing difficulties, it's easy to find yourself back in the conditioned patterns of arguing or trying to score points. Perhaps you're the kind of person who hides away and pushes all those negative feelings down and tries to ignore them as best you can until you feel like exploding.

It's during challenging times like this where you'll need to remind yourself about the power of Hoodoo magic and what it can do for you. It all starts with intention.

No matter what you're doing, what aspect of your life you're working with, or what spells you're practicing, the power of your actions will rely on the intentions behind them. For now, focus on how Hoodoo magic can help you.

There's perhaps a reason you picked up this book in the first place and a reason why you wanted to try Hoodoo magic. Let this guide you into opening yourself up to what's possible.

When you're getting started with your own connection to Hoodoo, this openness is what you will need to focus on most. Throughout the following pages of this book, from the next chapter onwards, we're going to be exploring the ins and outs of certain conjuring, protection, and healing spells, as well as some of the substances and natural products that have Hoodoo effects.

Preparing for Your Journey

We've covered the mindset aspects of readying yourself for your journey into Hoodoo, but now let's get a little more practical. While Hoodoo is a practice about connecting to the supernatural, there are some physical actions you need to take, such as collecting and working with objects and materials.

Most of these are simple, natural products that African-Americans would have had access to back in the 16th Century, such as plants, candles, leaves, bits of metal, and other magical trinkets like divination cards or totems.

Personal concerns are also commonly used in spells, especially when the spells or potions are directed at someone specific. Such concerns include things like locks of hair, nail clippings, blood, pieces of bone, or other forms of bodily fluids. Of course, you're not expecting to acquire a piece of bone from someone. This kind of spell would have been used to help someone who died while suffering to have a peaceful transition out of the physical realm into the spiritual realm.

Nevertheless, you want to start focusing on building up your collection of natural products and concerns from people you want to cast spells on, as well as containers. Some common products you'll want to collect include;

- Glass vials and bottles for storing potions

- Purses and fabric pouches for storing powders and grounded materials

- Candles of any color and design

- Matches or a lighter to light candles or burn spell components

- A pen and paper (or a special Hoodoo notebook) for writing down spells and intentions

- An assortment of plant roots and natural herbs

- Stones, minerals, and crystals

- Divination materials like incense, pinnacles, or tarot cards

- Oils, wax, amulets, charms, clothing, incense, and pendants

- The hair, bodily fluids, or concerns from yourself or another person

On this note, I do highly recommend getting yourself a special notebook for recording all your Hoodoo practices. Not only can you write down the spells and intentions you want to focus on, but also notes on your experience. You can write down how you feel and how spells worked for you, or perhaps what you would do differently next time.

Having this journey written down is invaluable because it will help you become a better and better practitioner, thus improving your skills, conjuring, and casting abilities, and will ultimately enhance your Hoodoo experiences tenfold.

When you start learning the spells themselves and begin having a preference for the kind of spells and potions you want to work with, you can start becoming a little more familiar with the ingredients you want, but it's always a good idea to keep an eye open for potential materials you could use.

And when you have your materials in place, you're ready to begin.

CHAPTER THREE

Introducing the Art of Conjuring

"If people don't face the danger that's seeking them, evil will find them first."

I experimented for well over a year with different spells and ways of using Hoodoo magic, trying to figure out what worked for me and what didn't, and no matter what I tried, I always ended up back in the same place with the same kind of spells. These were conjuring spells, or manifestation spells, as they are sometimes referred to.

There are different beliefs as to what these kinds of spells can do and their limits, but at their core, the power and intention of these spells remain the same and, therefore, can be used in many different ways. To conjure or to manifest is to put something that doesn't exist into your physical world through the power of intentions, thoughts, willingness, and belief.

Now, this, of course, doesn't mean that you can simply close your eyes and manifest a million dollars to appear in front of you in a shiny black briefcase. The physical world is bound by limitations that prevent this from happening and being possible, but that doesn't mean you can't manifest a million dollars into your life in other ways. This kind of conjuring would be more along the lines of conjuring financial security and comfort.

To conjure something in your life is to put yourself in a mindset where you can make it happen. You are literally going through the process of conjuring what you want and bringing it into your life. Throughout your life, you may think about conjuring:

- The relationships you want

- The career you want

- Financial security

- The house or car you want

- A promotion you want

- The completion of a dream you've always had, such as writing a book or running a marathon

The list of possibilities is endless, and you're only limited by your imagination. In my own life, I manifested the focus and creativity to write this book. I managed to protect and help myself heal from the trauma of my past relationships. I've promoted good fortune when going for job interviews, approaching new clients, and meeting new people.

When I've felt stressed, anxious, or overwhelmed, I've used Hoodoo to bring myself back to a grounded state of mind and found new and creative ways to overcome the obstacles and difficult situations I've found myself in. This was all achieved through the power of Hoodoo conjuration spells.

Conjuration literally means to cast a magic spell or incantation. In Hoodoo, this is to create a connection to the spiritual realm, allowing supernatural forces to enter your life and create an effect that will positively benefit you. This could be manifesting good luck, shielding yourself from harm, and so on.

It really doesn't matter what you want in your life, Hoodoo is a way of helping you get from A to B and turning your intentions into your reality, all thanks to the help of supernatural forces, spirits, and entities. To cast a spell is to connect with these beings, communicating and conjuring their presence into life, depending on what you're trying to achieve.

So, how does this work, and how do you cast such conjuring spells? Let's look at a detailed example of how the Hoodoo conjuration process works and then some of the ways you can introduce these spells into your own life.

Imagine you wake up one day, and you're in a fantastic mood.

You're well-rested and energized, and you're looking forward to a great day. Because you're in such a good mood, you start asking yourself what you want to achieve for the day. Because you want to achieve these goals, you take time to cast a spell of good fortune, thus increasing your luck for whatever situations you find yourself in.

Through the act of casting the spell, you've set a message out to the supernatural forces of the universe to come to you to assist you in your endeavors. As the day goes on, you'll find yourself in increasingly more favorable situations.

Perhaps you'll receive an email you've been waiting for. Maybe your boss will have a meeting you've been waiting for about a promotion, or a client will get back to you about your proposal. These are the supernatural forces at work, slightly pulling on the strings behind the scenes to ensure everything aligns when it needs to, mostly in the tiniest ways that we could never comprehend.

As you set out into your day, you're thinking about these goals, and your brain is focused on making them happen. Anything that comes your way, whether things, people, or experiences, that will help you take a step towards the fulfillment of these goals, you'll treat them with gratitude and compassion.

This is all thanks to the guidance of supernatural forces ensuring you're in the right place at the right time, and their impact outside your immediate reality.

Of course, conjuration magic doesn't have to be used in such a subtle way or for such a 'positive' reason. If you were in a friendship, but your friend did something really hurtful to you, such as sleeping with your partner, spreading rumors about you, or ruining your reputation, you could conjure supernatural forces to address this issue.

You can use the magic to conjure a protective shield around yourself, heal a wound (physical or emotional) that has been created from the situation, or even redirecting the negative energy back at the person who sent it to you in the first place, giving them a taste of what they're doing, hopefully teaching them the lesson not to do it again.

The act of conjuration is literally to conjure or summon spirits to assist you in your life. How you summon the spirit will determine the spirit that helps and for what purpose it's going to serve you. As you'll see later on in the book, this usually involves some kind of ritual and magical practice, as well as ingredients and spell components, as we spoke about before.

From influencing people to fall in love with you, opening up new opportunities, protecting yourself, becoming more creative, or healing pains, Hoodoo magic provides a solution.

And with that, you should know everything you need to know when it comes to solidly understanding what Hoodoo and rootwork are all about. Now it's time to take a proper first step into this new world.

CHAPTER FOUR

Rootwork Spells for Conjuring and Manifestation

"One you'll soon learn is that while preparations for a spell can be complicated, the spells themselves will be quite easy to perform. "

For now, that's enough theorizing. It's time to get into the practical part of this book. With your mind open and your intentions to learn the techniques and conjure fresh in your mind, it's time to connect to Hoodoo power and channel it into your day-to-day life.

Bear in mind that some of the spells and their ingredients may sound a little complicated, or it feels like there's a lot of little bits and pieces you'll need to collect. It can take some time to build up your collection of magical items but note that many components can be used interchangeably among spells. Once you have access to a component, chances are you'll be using it for many years to come.

Now, allow me to show you the way.

Incense: The Most Common Way to Conjure

Spells can be difficult to put together, especially when you need to collect all the components, but there is an obvious way you can cast a small conjuring spell at any time, and that's by burning incense.

There are countless forms of incense out there, and you can almost perform the spell as a kind of mediation. All you need is an incense holder, preferably with an ash catcher, and whatever kind of incense you want to burn.

Simply place your incense in the holder, light it, and sit with it for a few minutes. The longer you sit and essentially meditate with the burning incense, the more powerful the spell, and therefore your intention, will be. Just sit with it, smell the aromas, and mindfully try to connect with that Hoodoo power source within you and within the universe.

As you sit, breathing deeply, stay as present as possible, and try to nudge your mind in the direction of your intentions. Take a moment to think about what you want and some of the ways you could go about getting it. Don't try to be solid with your reason, but rather let your instinct flow and see what comes to mind. Be fluid, like water. See what comes up and release your conditioned ways of thinking.

For example, you might try to think of some ways to be happier and more motivated at work, but as you think about it, you start to realize you're actually not in a job you want to be in, and instead you want to pursue a more fulfilling career. This kind of realization is the Hoodoo magic at work, so allow it to be, rather than dismissing it as hopeful thinking.

With that, here are some of the types of incense you may want to look into for conjuring and helping to increase and improve your focus and intention.

- Palo Santo is great if you're looking to heal something in your life. It's said to increase your energy vibrations and calm your body.

- Frankincense is ideal if you're looking to relieve stress and gain more awareness. If you're struggling and feel lost, this is the incense to help bring clarity.

- If you're seeking success and prosperity, you can burn Star Anise or Cinnamon incense to help bring you into a state of mind where you're making the best decisions in this area.

- Lavender is the incense of balance. If you need calm, clarity, and peace for setting intentions, discovering them, or reconnecting with yourself or the Hoodoo source, this is an excellent incense for clearing the mind and remaining grounded during turbulent times.

- Use Copal if you're looking for a deeper connection to yourself, the Hoodoo source, or the universe. This is the incense used for transcending or deepening the spiritual connections you already have.

- If you're looking for a tremendous all-rounded incense that attracts a bit of everything, you'll need some Cinquefoil. While not powerful, this is a fantastic pick-me-up incense or to help you stay motivated if you're already in a positive place.

The intensity and impact of incense spells can vary dramatically. Sometimes it can feel subtle, while other times, the effect can feel life-changing. It really depends on the experience, the incense, and where you are in your headspace.

However, if you're looking for something a little more powerful, consistent, and more dedicated, then you're going to want to use a spell. Shared below are some relatively beginner-friendly casts.

The Luck Draw Mojo

The Luck Draw Mojo spell is used to attract money into your life, be it through increased luck or good fortune. For example, if you're quoting a job to a new client and you want to aim high, or you're asking your boss for a pay rise, this is the kind of spell that will help you successfully secure the finances you're looking for.

Ingredients

- A red flannel pouch

- Magnetic sand

- A clove of garlic

- A lodestone

- Some sugar

- Some whiskey

Place both the lodestone and the garlic into the flannel pouch, pour in a shot of whiskey. Close it up and sprinkle some magnetic sand and sugar onto the pouch itself. Sew the pouch shut. As you go through this process, ensure you're speaking your intentions aloud.

The Serenity Spell

Life can feel turbulent, even at the best of times. This is why for many of us, it is important to take some time to find our peace, to return to a grounded state of mind, and just generally look after your health and wellbeing. Taking the time to perform a serenity spell is perfect for this, and it's relatively simple.

Ingredients

- 12 white candles

Wait until a full moon night and light all 12 candles in a circle around you. Sit comfortably for as long or as little as you like. While sitting, focus on your breathing and being present and grounded at the moment. Let the stress, anxieties, and worries fade away into nothingness as the moonlight, and the universal energy cleanses you and your being.

A Spell for Protection

No Hoodoo magic book would be complete without a protection spell. It's one of the most powerful and most universally applicable spells. Whether you're heading into a tough conversation, an emotionally draining situation, a hard time, or you're just looking out for yourself and your headspace, a protection spell can work wonders.

Fortunately, it's one of the simplest spells to perform. You need no ingredients or components. Just you and the words. Just say this spell to yourself, in your head or out loud, whenever you need it:

Pater noster dei sanctorum. Maria bella angelorum. Beautiful Mary sleeping. And the baby Jesus appeared to her in a dream. Dear, I dreamt that at the ordeal they brought you. Golden crowns lifted you up, and thorns have planted you. What you are saying is truth, the Christ answered to your mother. And whoever says this three times in a field is not afraid. Water, Thunder, and Lightning.

Just repeat whenever you need access to the protection. As you can tell from the cursive of the spells, this is a spell to help you not be afraid, no matter what you're facing, and that you're protected by the beings and spirits that are greater than you as an individual.

A Spell for Passion

Don't confuse this with a love spell. A passion spell is a way of increasing the connection and passion in an already-existing relationship, ideally between you and your romantic lover.

Ingredients

- Lavender Oil (3 Drops)

- Hot Sauce (3 Drops)

- Orris root pieces

- Whole peppercorns

- Three cups of rainwater

This spell is very easy to perform. What's more, you can essentially scale it up as much as you like. You can make as much or as little as you like, as long as you're using the ratios listed in the ingredients.

Take your ingredients and pour everything into a bowl and stir. While stirring, draw your attention to the heat of the hot sauce (the hotter the sauce, the more intense the spell will be), and focus on the temperatures and textures. If there are any smells, then this is what you'll want to focus on.

After everything has been stirred together well, take some of the mixture and sprinkle it at the front door to your house, or an entrance to a room or apartment. Cover this area well, and be sure to add some to the walkway. Now the lovers passing over this entrance will be driven by the increase in passion suggested to them by the supernatural forces you've invited to work alongside you.

With that, we draw to the end of this fine chapter. At this point, you have started a beautiful collection of spells that you can dip into and use to connect to the Hoodoo source whenever you need to. As for now, these spells should allow you to connect with your intentions (as well as helping to define them) with clarity, helping you in any situation or experience that you find yourself in.

Now it's time to move on to something a little more powerful.

CHAPTER FIVE

Rootwork Potions

"All hold that the Bible is the great conjure book in the world."

The final step in your introduction to Hoodoo magic still resides within the magical sphere of the practice, but this time focuses on the power of potions and other spells. These spells tend to lean more into the practice of rootwork and what you can expect from such a practice. Choose the ones you like as a starting point, but don't be afraid to try something new and branch out.

These are all potions and rootwork recipes passed down since Hoodoo was first established, but they serve as an entry point. There are certainly simpler and more complex recipes out there, so embrace the knowledge and dive in.

A Potion for Happiness

If you're looking for a way to boost your mood, to help you think more positively, and to help you focus on more productive outcomes, this is a potion that could benefit you greatly.

Ingredients

- A small potion pot, ideally with a cap or lid

- A dried and crushed dandelion

- One tablespoon of oregano (powder form)

- One tablespoon of cinnamon (powder form)

- One tablespoon of thyme powder

- Seven pine needles

Add all the ingredients into the potion pot, vial, container, or ampoule, and close it. Then, kneel facing East and hold the container in your hands to perform the spell, reciting Psalm no.7 seven times. It reads:

O LORD my God, I take refuge in you; save and deliver me from all who pursue me,

or they will tear me like a lion and rip me to pieces with no one to rescue me.

O LORD my God, if I have done this and there is guilt on my hands--

if I have done evil to him who is at peace with me or without cause have robbed my foe--

then let my enemy pursue and overtake me; let him trample my life to the ground and make me sleep in the dust. Selah

Arise, O LORD, in your anger; rise up against the rage of my enemies. Awake, my God; decree justice.

Let the assembled peoples gather around you. Rule over them from on high;

let the LORD judge the peoples. Judge me, O LORD, according to my righteousness, according to my integrity, O Most High.

O righteous God, who searches minds and hearts, bring to an end the violence of the wicked and make the righteous secure.

My shield[l] is God Most High, who saves the upright in heart.

God is a righteous judge, a God who expresses his wrath every day.

If he does not relent, he will sharpen his sword; he will bend and string his bow.

He has prepared his deadly weapons; he makes ready his flaming arrows.

He who is pregnant with evil and conceives trouble gives birth to disillusionment.

He who digs a hole and scoops it out falls into the pit he has made.

The trouble he causes recoils on himself; his violence comes down on his own head.

I will give thanks to the LORD because of his righteousness and will sing praise to the name of the LORD Most High.

This spell does take a little bit of time to cast and clearly comes from Christian origins, but after you've created the potion, you've got it indefinitely. Just take the vial around with you wherever you go, and it will bring you good luck while attracting happiness.

A Protection Spell for Your Home

If you are experiencing turbulent times at home, stressful or emotionally distressing situations, or the peace and wellbeing of your home are otherwise in jeopardy, then you can significantly benefit from this spell.

Ingredients

- A glass jar with an airtight lid

- Some broken glass

- Nail clippings from yourself or an animal (such as your pet)

- Some plugs

- Some glass wool

- A thistle

- Some Absinthe

Also, collect these components that you won't place in the jar:

- A pentacle of banishment or red felt to make one

- A consecrated black candle

- Banishing oil

Put all the ingredients listed above inside the glass jar and seal it. Place a pentacle of banishment on the lid. You can make a pentacle by cutting one out of red felt or using one you already have. Place the black candle dressed with banishing oil on the lid on top of the pentacle and light said candle. Now recite the following incantation:

Black candle and old curses, release your powers, reverse the flow of spells cast, leave pain and sorrow in the past.

Let the candle completely burn out. When it has, take the jar and bury it somewhere near your home, as close as you can get. If performed correctly and with intention, you will experience a protective shield around your home that should last up to six months. When the spell's power starts to diminish, simply repeat the process with a new jar.

A Potion for Prosperity

This is a powerful potion spell if you're seeking ways to boost success in any area of your life, whether in your career, personal missions, relationships, health, and wellbeing, or any other area of your life that you want to focus on.

Peace and prosperity are welcome and necessary in everybody's life, certainly at some point or another, and with this potion, you're sure to attract the right intentions that can help lead you to it.

Ingredients

- A jar (conventional glass jar will do)

- Three green and three gold candles

- Rosemary, bay, basil, thyme, lavender, and clove leaves (seven of each)

- Oil

- Three silver coins (any currency)

- A stick (wooden)

The recipe for this potion is relatively simple. Add all the herb leaves together into the jar, along with the coins, and cover everything in the oil. Then create a circle around the jar with the candles, alternating the colors as you go. Now light them.

Using the stick, mix the contents of the jar clockwise for seven rotations while reciting the magic words. Repeat this sequence of phrases seven times.

Paisa. Panam. Pecuina. Penz. Para. Dirua.

Now mix the jar contents in the opposite direction and repeat the next sequence of phrases seven times.

Aurid. Arap. Znep. Manap. Asia.

Now break the stick you were using to mix in half and put it in the jar, and leave the mixture in the circle, letting the candles burn out. Once they are gone, leave the jar somewhere in your house for it to bring prosperity into your home.

A Potion for Relationships (For Love and Friendship)

Your relationships are one of the most impactful areas of your life. In most aspects of this human existence, it's not what you know that will determine where you go and where life takes you, but who you know. It's the presence of others that will either raise you up to new heights or will hold you back profoundly. That's why it can be so special to develop a potion to help you attract love and friendship from the right people.

Ingredients

- Rosewater

- Three strawberries

- Three vanilla pods

- Three tablespoons of cocoa

- Three tablespoons of salt

- A saucepan

- A bottle (usually glass)

- A single sheet of people

- A red marker pen

Put your saucepan on your hob and place all your ingredients (minus your pen, paper, and bottle) into the pan, boiling for 30 minutes on a low heat setting. Now take your paper and, using your red marker, write the words:

"Pure love. Strong love. Open all the doors to me. Pure love. Strong friendship. Luck be favorable to me."

Roll up the paper when you're done and put it in the glass bottle before filtering the saucepan contents and pouring the now-soaked rose water liquid into the bottle as well. Close the bottle to ensure none of the content escapes.

From here, hold the bottle in your hands, shake it back and forth, and repeat the phrase that you wrote down seven times over.

A Potion for Making Someone Fall in Love with You

This may sound a little strange, but this is an effective spell that can be used in various situations for different reasons. The first that comes to mind is wanting someone to fall in love with you and want to be with you. While this is entirely possible with this spell (although I would recommend using the spell with care and caution), there are other uses you can consider.

For example, if your partner is stuck in an old way of thinking, is stressed, or isn't listening to you properly, they lack the compassion and empathy to keep the relationship balanced. This is a spell that can help remind them. If you seek forgiveness, this spell can help nudge their intention in this direction.

Ingredients

- A bottle of salt

- A few strands (a lock) of hair from the person you want the spell to resonate with

- Nine red, green, and yellow candles (nine of each)

Use the salt to create a circle of salt large enough for you to sit comfortably in and place the candles around the circle's edge, alternating the color with every candle, going from green to yellow to red, and so on.

Now sit in the circle and take your time lighting the candles one at a time, starting with the candle sitting in the most Eastern direction. In your right hand, hold the lock of hair and close your eyes. Say their name 99 times, making sure you picture the person as clearly as you possibly can in your mind's eye.

Let the candles burn out, and keep the same lock of hair in your pillowcase where you sleep for as long as you like.

Ishtar's Love Connection

Another spell you can cast to connect and form bonds of love with people in your life is by using Ishtar's Love Ligament spell. Ishtar is an ancient goddess in Mesopotamian religions, known as the goddess of war and sexual love. To cast a spell in her name is to draw on this ancient power to bring about love in your own life, to invoke love, compassion, and peace in others.

If you're looking for love in any area of your life, then this is a powerful, long-lasting spell that can create such an impact.

Ingredients

- A one-meter-long piece of red silk ribbon

Every night, for 48 nights in a row, tie a single knot in your silk ribbon while reciting the following incantation;

In the name of Ishtar, the one who makes everything fruitful, I tie you to me, and your love for me day by day as ivy on the wall will grow. So be it. So it will be.

On day 49, at dawn, as the sun starts to break the horizon, travel to a crossroads in a rural area or a place that you know to be connected with Hoodoo ancestry, and burn the ribbon, scattering the ashes into the wind.

The Powerful Negra Cinta

Personally, I don't condone using powerful Black magic spells on others. However, circumstances differ from person to person, and you may have reasons for performing such a spell. I am not here to judge, but I highly recommend that you move forward with extreme caution. I included this spell specifically for educational reasons but will not share others for safety reasons.

The Negra Cinta is a powerful Black magic Hoodoo spell that's designed for revenge. At the advent of Hoodoo magic, Black people would perform this on those causing significant harm, such as a slave owner or traders. It's a spell that redirects pain, trauma and suffering back at those who perpetrate it. However, it's an incredibly difficult spell to pull off due to how powerful its effects can be.

Ingredients

- A black candle

- A sheet of rolling cigarette paper

- Scorpion oil (alacran oil)

- Snake fat

- A black pin and black ink

- A parrot feather

- A black ribbon or black belt

- Black salt

- Cemetery land or a place connected with Hoodoo origins

You must ensure you're following the steps of this spell to the letter to ensure it's performed correctly. Start by engraving the name of the person you're placing the spell on onto the candle, using a knife of some kind. Pour the scorpion oil onto the engraving and sprinkle some black salt on it.

Let the candle sit for several hours upright before lighting it. Place a map of the person's geographical location of the person you're placing the spell on next to the candle, and write down the wishes, requests, curses, or actions you want taken against this person. Be sure to write them with the parrot feather and the black ink.

This is the part of the spell you want to perform carefully, making sure you're writing down what you want. You may want to show them the error of their ways, make them realize how horrible or nasty they have been, for them to experience how much pain they have caused, or whatever you want. Just write it on the map.

Now, cover the map with the snake fat and leave the set up alone until the candle has been burned completely. After that, fold up the map and hold it closed with the black ribbon, making sure to tie the ribbon in a knot seven times. Close the final knot with the black pin. As you tie each and every knot, you need to recite the following passage (totaling seven repetitions):

Forces of evil that since the times of times you rule the destinies of men, I invoke you to subdue with all your immense strength, every thought, word, and work of NN, that all go wrong to him, that no one listens to his cry and that all the evil that has caused me to return back to him/her and his/her family multiplied by 100. And so be it.

Once the candle has burned out, collect the remains alongside with your map, wrap everything together with the ribbon and the pin that should hold all the components together. Now bury everything far away from anything else on cemetery land. The spell will then start to take effect as the magic begins to flow.

There's a vast range of resources and information on other spells you can perform and what kind of incantations are possible, and it's all waiting for you to explore. For now, you have a solid platform to get started and experiment with what Hoodoo magic is capable of.

Now move forward, get started on this journey, and discover what the magic of Hoodoo can do for you.

Conclusion

The entire idea behind Hoodoo magic is to help you channel the power that already exists inside you in a productive way that benefits you, connecting you to the rest of the universe and the universal powers that be. Remember, this is magic that can be used in all areas of your life, whether you're trying to improve your luck, find prosperity, peace, better relationships, or clarity.

In essence, the core of Hoodoo is to improve your everyday life through intentions. This is achieved by accessing and connecting with yourself and your inner power and the power of our ancestors and our history. It's an incredible thing, and even if you're dubious, it's one of those practices that will get better in time, and the more you practice and open your mind to what's possible, the more you'll start to see the effects in your day-to-day life.

This book serves as an introduction to get you started, but the world of Hoodoo magic goes far deeper than what we've discussed. Once you've become familiar with the basics outlined in this book, you can continue with your explorations.

This means reading more books, specifically spell books, to further understand what you're able to achieve. It also means diving into your own exploration of the practice. Whether it is writing about your experiences, meditating, or tuning in to your own feelings and instincts, there's a lot you can discover by looking within yourself. If you have an instinctual drive to create a potion or to cast a spell that suits you, and you can feel the core of Hoodoo magic burning within you and nudging you in the direction of clarity, then more often than not, you're going to want to follow this lead.

Learn to trust yourself and your instincts. They can show you the world.

Remember, intentional thinking and practicing hoodoo magic can be a compelling and impactful journey. It can change your life, so make sure you're treating the knowledge, your own journey, and the experiences of others with respect and care. It would be foolish to underestimate what you can learn by traveling down this path.

For now, that's all from me. I hope you enjoyed this book and you learned something from it, and in some way, found some benefit in the text. If you did, then I would appreciate hearing back from you. You can do this by leaving a review on the site where you purchased your copy. For me, any feedback means the world and helps me to become the best version of myself, so I look forward to reading everything you have to say.

From here, I wish you all the best in the future, especially with your spiritual and magical endeavors. Good luck, and keep your mind open to learning and all the new possibilities that come with it. Until next time!

BOOK #3

Shadow Work Journal

37 Days of Guided Prompts and Exercises for Self-Discovery, Emotional Triggers, Inner Child Healing, and Authentic Growth

Introduction

To be honest, this was supposed to be another type of journal. My initial idea for this book was to focus on the things that make you uncomfortable and how to push yourself out of that zone.

But I was suddenly invited to a barbecue backyard party at my friend's house, where I spent a good 10 minutes watching his one-year-old trying to catch his shadow. Almost like a dog relentlessly chasing his tail, he was making circles in the sun, getting frustrated with how he couldn't touch something that he could clearly see.

You can guess where the story ended, with a high-pitch cry and him dropping his ice cream, but let's leave that story for a "how to shift attention in toddlers" conversation. What he did in the sun got me thinking about our shadow and gave this journal a whole new meaning.

It's always right there behind us, our shadow. Regardless of where you are in the world, shed some light on your physical figure, at it will cast a shadow. But did you know that there is also one inside of you?

Every one of us hides a darker side. Maybe you are not aware of it yet, maybe you are suppressing it because it brings out discomfort, but it is right there inside. Embedded in your psyche, waiting to come out and bring the worst in you.

This journal will not only help you dig deep and acknowledge its presence, but it will also challenge it so that you can work on the things that make you uncomfortable and maybe cause pain.

With these shadow work prompts, you will get in touch with the parts of your unconsciousness that you have repressed for so long and allow yourself the chance to be free from the shackles of the darkness within.

All you have to do is answer honestly, and who you truly are will help you get to who you really want to be.

The Darker You

"Everyone carries a shadow, and the less it is embodied in the individual's conscious life, the blacker and denser it is"
– Carl Jung

As we grow up, with every act we perform and every decision we make, we slowly add pieces of the puzzles that form our personality. And as we go through this process, we learn that some parts of our behavior are better than others.

Those parts of our personality that are considered good are then rewarded and celebrated by our parents, caregivers, teachers... This can be an act of kindness, the ability to solve problems, or showing artistic predispositions. Once we learn our traits, we proudly put them on display for others to see.

The things that we, as kids, were maybe scolded for, punished, or criticized, we associate with bad behavior. This can be our anger, sadness, impulsiveness, or even sexuality. These are the parts of our personality that we deny or maybe feel ashamed of. They are the ones we put in a vault inside, leaving them forever ignored.

And this may seem like a good thing. After all, who would like to show others that losing a single poker hand makes them turn the table over and punch the wall? But here's the catch. The more you repress your feelings to hide fear, shame, pain, or anxiety, the harder they come back. Think of pressing on an inflated ball underwater. The harder you push, the quicker it will slip from your hands and turn sideways.

So, where's the shadow in all of this? According to Carl Jung, the inner shadow consists of all the things that you reject about yourself. All of the feelings that are churning inside but you don't let out. From *I am not sad that my ex-partner has moved on* to *I don't mind you chewing with your mouth open* types of delusions.

Meeting Your Shadow Self

Your shadow, as all shadows do, follows you around every step of the way. Know that it is there, and you will be able to tap into your fears and insecurities for an emotionally healthy life. Look the other way and ignore its presence, and it will turn against you.

Because here's the thing. Your shadow self doesn't really need your consciousness for it to operate. It can do so easily without your full awareness. Remember "Fight Club"? Edward Norton plays a character who is living his life in denial. Successful in the terms of a nice house and a job that pays the bills, but a huge piece inside of him is missing. He starts living his life in a foggy state, never fully present. Eventually, he forms an alter ego (Brad Pitt) who has all of the restrained desires and repressed traits that Edward Norton couldn't acknowledge. In this case, Brad Pitt is Edward Norton's shadow. And in the end, the shadow ends up nearly killing the conscious self.

We all have a shadow inside. We have just adjusted how we gratify what we need so we can adapt to our surroundings. Everything that was once discouraged or unacceptable, is now sitting in a pile inside causing us pain. Why? Because we are not aware of the reason for our pain.

And in the wise Jungian words, you can never be physically whole if you do not let yourself be imperfect, just like there is no light without a shadow.

Shadow Work and Why You Need It

So, how do I get rid of this shadow, some might think. Well, you don't! And you shouldn't want to! Acknowledging the presence of your shadow shouldn't be about making it disappear, but accepting why you're going through what you're going through.

Your shadow may come to you in the form of anger outbursts, negative self-talk, sadness, depression, fear, or other self-sabotaging actions. And the only way in which we can overcome these self-destructing feelings is by understanding why they have come to the surface in the first place.

Shadow work is about dragging your unconscious self (repressed thoughts and emotions) to your conscious awareness. It is what the most psychoanalytic minds such as Jung and Freud believed was the number one priority for being psychologically healthy.

Doing shadow work can help you:

- Become more intuitive

- Accept your strengths

- Work on your weaknesses

- Find a greater purpose in life

- Find meaning in the smallest of things

- Empower yourself

- Improve your self-confidence

- Gain psychological freedom

Shadow work is usually approached in the Socratic way. That means that the best way to explore the things that you push down inside is to answer objective questions in the most subjective way possible. You will need to go back in the past, rethink old actions, reexamine stories, and basically, dig up some bones.

This will not only be challenging but at times will feel extremely uncomfortable. So please, when answering the questions in this workbook, try not to stage your answers or fake your emotions. Remember, these are YOUR prompts and will be written and read solely by YOU. If you do not wish to share your thoughts with another person, you don't have to. That's not what this is about. The point is for you to be truthful with yourself, as that is the only way for you to understand what the *shadow you* is causing to your *conscious self.*

Because of the amount of discomfort that you might experience along the way, I highly suggest you take this one prompt at a time. Answer one question a day, and in just 37 days, you will let go of the pain and start being less judgmental to your actions.

Day 1

The Hidden Feelings

Think about a time when being around someone made you feel uncomfortable. You know, those times when you try so hard not to show your emotions, but inside you are bursting without even knowing why. Write down the name of the person and explain the situation you were in. Talk about the feelings you were experiencing. At the very bottom, list three possible reasons that you think caused you to feel that way.

_____

_____

_____

_____

_____

_____

_____

_____

_____

_____

_____

_____

_____

_____

_____

_____

_____

_____

_____

_____

_____

_____

_____

_____

_____

_____

_____

_____

_____

_____

_____

_____

_____

_____

_____

_____

_____

_____

_____

_____

_____

_____

_____

_____

_____

_____

"Whatever makes you uncomfortable is your biggest opportunity for growth" – Bryant McGill

Day 2

The Mental Delete Button

Is there something from your memory that you wish you could forget? Imagine that you have a "delete" button in your brain, and the power to delete a single memory from it. What would you choose? What memory causes you the most pain? Write about that memory here and explain the feelings that it creates. At the bottom, write about how you think you might feel if that memory never existed.

_____

_____

_____

_____

_____

_____

_____

_____

_____

_____

_____

_____

_____

_____

_____

_____

_____

_____

_____

_____

_____

_____

_____

_____

_____

_____

_____

_____

_____

_____

_____

_____

_____

_____

_____

_____

_____

_____

_____

_____

_____

_____

_____

_____

_____

_____

_____

_____

_____

_____

"One cannot and must not try to erase the past merely because it does not fit the present" – Golda Mer

Day 3

The Letter to Your Child-Self

If you could go back in time and face your child-self, what advice would you have given to the young version of yourself? Write down all the things that you wish you would have known as a child. Make sure to address things that caused you pain and sadness. Now read aloud. Could you actually use some of that advice today?

_____

_____

_____

_____

_____

_____

_____

_____

_____

_____

_____

_____

_____

_____

_____

_____

_____

_____

_____

_____

_____

_____

_____

_____

"If we cannot alter the time of events, at least we can be nearby with towels to mop up" – Peter David

Day 4

The Offended One

Think about a time when you felt the most offended. Who offended you? What words do they use? How did that make you feel? Explain the situation in detail, but try to focus more on the emotions involved in the process. Was that person angry? Scared? What was your reaction?

_____

_____

_____

_____

_____

_____

_____

_____

_____

_____

_____

_____

_____

_____

_____

_____

_____

_____

_____

_____

_____

_____

_____
_____
_____
_____
_____
_____
_____
_____
_____
_____
_____
_____
_____
_____
_____
_____
_____
_____
_____
_____
_____
_____
_____
_____
_____
_____
_____

"The feeling of being offended is a warming indicator that is showing you where to look within yourself for unresolved issues" – Bryant McGill

Day 5

The Toxic Relationships

Do all relationships in your life feel good? If so, was there ever a time when you were in a toxic relationship? Try to explain some negative aspects of your relationship with someone in your life, whether a partner, friend or even a family member. How does/did being with that person make you feel? What is/was it about that relationship that you think is/was the most toxic?

_____

_____

_____

_____

_____

_____

_____

_____

_____

_____

_____

_____

_____

_____

_____

_____

_____

_____

_____

_____

"You should not set yourself on fire to keep others warm" – Unknown

Day 6

The Biggest Fears

We are all afraid of something, we just have to realize what it is so we can work our way around and eventually face it. What are you afraid of? Try to think about the top three things that scare you the most in life. Write them down. Why are you afraid of them? What kind of emotions do these things drag with them?

_____

_____

_____

_____

_____

_____

_____

_____

_____

_____

_____

_____

_____

_____

_____

_____

_____

_____

_____

_____

_____

_____

_____

"Bravery is not being afraid to be afraid" – Marie Colvin

Day 7

The Mask

Do you ever find yourself acting against your emotions? Do you ever take on another persona when you are around a certain person? Who are you with when you find yourself being another person? Think about why you do that. Is it to impress someone? To cover up for your lack of confidence? Lack of knowledge? What do you think would happen if you showed your real face? How does acting differently make you feel inside?

_____

_____

_____

_____

_____

_____

_____

_____

_____

_____

_____

_____

_____

_____

_____

_____

_____

_____

_____

_____

"Learn how to love yourself just as much as you want to be loved" – Unknown

Day 8

The Shame

What are you most ashamed of? Dig really deep and try to include as many details as possible. Imagine a certain situation where you would feel embarrassed. Can you explain it? If nothing specific comes to mind, think about a time when you felt ashamed. What caused you to feel that way? How did you cope with shame? What were your reactions?

_____

_____

_____

_____

_____

_____

_____

_____

_____

_____

_____

_____

_____

_____

_____

_____

_____

_____

_____

_____

_____

_____

"Stop being ashamed of how many times you've fallen, and start being proud of how many times you've got up" – Unknown

Day 9

The Negative Traits

How would you not want to be described? What are the worst possible traits that you could think of? Don't just list negative characteristics, mention them in terms of your personality. For instance, if you had a fight with your partner over not wanting to participate in activities that interested them, the worst attribute they might give you could be "selfish." Explain how these negative traits make you feel? Would it be terrible if someone called you that?

_____

_____

_____

_____

_____

_____

_____

_____

_____

_____

_____

_____

_____

_____

_____

_____

_____

_____

_____

_____

"Spiteful words can hurt your feelings, but silence breaks your heart" – C. S. Lewis

Day 10

The Comparison

Think about how you see yourself in comparison to other people. Do you think of yourself being less worthy? Do you feel equal? Or do you think you're somehow superior? Add a <u>WHY</u> to that question and answer what causes you to feel that way. Also, try to name the people that make you feel less worthy or superior? Why do you think that is? Explore this in detail.

_____

_____

_____

_____

_____

_____

_____

_____

_____

_____

_____

_____

_____

_____

_____

_____

_____

_____

_____

_____

_____

_____

_____
_____
_____
_____
_____
_____
_____
_____
_____
_____
_____
_____
_____
_____
_____
_____
_____
_____
_____
_____
_____
_____
_____
_____
_____

"A lot of doubt and uncertainties in our lives come from not knowing that we are worthy" – Unknown

Day 11

The Trigger

When was the last time that you lost your temper? When was the last time that you wished you would have lost your temper? Why? What triggers you to have such strong emotions? Explain the situations in detail, and think about this. What is different between these two situations? When do you feel free to allow yourself to express your feelings, and when do you think you need to suppress everything inside?

_____

"Triggers are unresolved feelings causing us to overreact" – Unknown

Day 12

The Bad Habit

Do you have any bad habits? Why are they bad? Do they interfere with other aspects of your life? Have other people recognized some of these habits? How do they feel about that? How does that make you feel? Be specific about the habits you think are destructive and how those actions impact your life.

_____

_____

_____

_____

_____

_____

_____

_____

_____

_____

_____

_____

_____

_____

_____

_____

_____

_____

_____

_____

_____

_____

_____

_____

_____

_____

_____

_____

_____

_____

_____

_____

_____

_____

_____

_____

_____

_____

_____

_____

_____

_____

_____

_____

_____

_____

_____

_____

_____

_____

"The truth is, you don't break a bad habit; you replace it with a new one" – Denis Waitley

Day 13

The Judge Control

Would you say you are a judgmental person? When was the last time you judged someone? Did you let that person know your thoughts or did you simply bury those feelings inside? What were you judging? If you cannot think of a specific example, make it up. Include a hypothetical situation where someone would behave in a way that you would judge.

_____

_____

_____

_____

_____

_____

_____

_____

_____

_____

_____

_____

_____

_____

_____

_____

_____

_____

_____

_____

_____

_____

_____

_____

_____

_____

_____

_____

_____

_____

_____

_____

_____

_____

_____

_____

_____

_____

_____

_____

_____

_____

_____

_____

_____

_____

"If we judge others, it is because we are judging something in ourselves of which we are unaware" – John A. Sanford

Day 14

The Unexplainable Feeling

Have you ever found yourself not being able to stand someone's actions/behavior, but not exactly knowing why? When we're unaware of why others' behavior flips us off, it is because that's a sheer reflection of emotions we're repressing. For instance, your cocky friend may get on your nerves because deep inside you hate yourself for not being able to have that much confidence. Explain a certain situation and spend some time trying to decipher what it means. Why do you experience these weird and disturbing feelings about that person? It might help to write down some of their traits and analyze them.

_____

_____

_____

_____

_____

_____

_____

_____

_____

_____

_____

_____

_____

_____

_____

_____

_____

_____

_____
_____
_____
_____
_____
_____
_____
_____
_____
_____
_____
_____
_____
_____
_____
_____
_____
_____
_____
_____
_____
_____
_____
_____
_____
_____
_____
_____

"All the repressed emotions and subconscious desires in time lead to some kind of psychological or physiological breakdown, if kept unchecked" – Abhijit Naskar

Day 15

The Values

What things are the most valuable to you? What do you cherish the most in this life? Write that down and explain why. Now, think about the people in life who don't share the same values as you. Can you think of a related experience? For instance, if you are quite a workaholic, this can be your partner/friend with a poor work ethic. How do you feel about that?

_____

_____

_____

_____

_____

_____

_____

_____

_____

_____

_____

_____

_____

_____

_____

_____

_____

_____

_____

_____

"It is not hard to make decisions when you know what your values are" – Roy Disney

Day 16

The Parents

Think about your parents or caregivers for a second. Write down the things you love about them. Now, think about all of their traits that you don't find so positive. How did these personality attributes impact your childhood and life in general? For instance, if your mother has always been unorganized, that might have something to do with you never learning how to manage your time. Do you think that these attributes are a direct contributor to some of your own negative traits? How does that make you feel?

_____

_____

_____

_____

_____

_____

_____

_____

_____

_____

_____

_____

_____

_____

_____

_____

_____

_____

_____

_____
_____
_____
_____
_____
_____
_____
_____
_____
_____
_____
_____
_____
_____
_____
_____
_____
_____
_____
_____
_____
_____
_____
_____
_____
_____

"There are no perfect parents, and there are no perfect children. But there are plenty of perfect moments along the way" – Dave Willis

Day 17

The Action

Is there a certain thing that you should be doing but aren't? What is stopping you from performing that action? Write it down. Are those things something that you can change? If so, why aren't you doing it? List all the reasons, no matter how scary or uncomfortable they may seem.

_____

_____

_____

_____

_____

_____

_____

_____

_____

_____

_____

_____

_____

_____

_____

_____

_____

_____

_____

_____

_____

_____

_____

_____

_____

_____

_____

_____

_____

_____

_____

_____

_____

_____

_____

_____

_____

_____

_____

_____

_____

_____

_____

_____

_____

_____

_____

"The only impossible journey is the one you never begin" – Tony Robbins

Day 18

The Victim

We have all been the victim in some aspects of our lives. This can be a victim of public prank or ridicule, or even something serious as physical abuse. What is the worst time in your life when you have been the victim? No matter how painful, write it down. Explain your feelings. Let this paper feel that you're hurt. And with every written word, imagine the shackles of the suffering loosening up. At the bottom of the page, write these words I AM NOW SAFE – I AM NOW FREE.

_____

_____

_____

_____

_____

_____

_____

_____

_____

_____

_____

_____

_____

_____

_____

_____

_____

_____

_____

_____

_____

"Every scar that you have is a reminder not just that you got hurt, but that you survived"
– Michelle Obama

Day 19

The Things I've Done

Every one of us can write lists of things we wish we have done differently. But how many things on that list would be really meaningful to you? Think about the worst thing you have done in your life. When did this take place and where? Who was with you? Who did you do this thing to? How did you feel right after doing this thing? What emotions come to you now, as you're writing about it?

_____

_____

_____

_____

_____

_____

_____

_____

_____

_____

_____

_____

_____

_____

_____

_____

_____

_____

_____

_____

_____

_____

_____

_____

_____

_____

_____

_____

_____

_____

_____

_____

_____

_____

_____

_____

_____

_____

_____

_____

_____

_____

_____

_____

_____

_____

_____

_____

"You are so much more than the worst thing you've done" – Greg Boyle

Day 20

The Mirror on the Wall

For this exercise, I suggest you grab a mirror. Stand in front of it, and look at your reflection for a few minutes. During this time, allow yourself to feel, and be yourself. Do not think about anything in particular. Do not try to answer inner questions. Just observe. If a thought pops into your head, acknowledge it, and let it go. Do not dwell. Just feel. Now, put down the mirror, and write down how you are feeling inside. Do not just say "sad," Explain what you think has triggered this emotion. Why?   Although you cannot see your shadow self in a mirror, this can be a great exercise for you to understand how the "darker you" is feeling.

_____

_____

_____

_____

_____

_____

_____

_____

_____

_____

_____

_____

_____

_____

_____

_____

_____

_____

_____

_____

_____

_____

_____

_____

_____

"Always be true to your feelings because the more you deny what you feel, the stronger it becomes" – Unknown

Day 21

The Regret

What is your biggest regret? Don't just think about things you wish to change; focus on the things that you have caused. For instance, deciding not to take that job abroad made sense at the time, but now it eats you up inside. Think about what your biggest regret feels like? Why? How would you feel if you actually made a different decision at the time? Do you think you would be happier and more content at the moment? Explain why. Now go through that "why list". Isn't there another way for you to achieve that?

_____

_____

_____

_____

_____

_____

_____

_____

_____

_____

_____

_____

_____

_____

_____

_____

_____

_____

_____

_____

_____

_____

_____

_____

_____

_____

_____

_____

_____

_____

_____

_____

_____

_____

_____

_____

_____

_____

_____

_____

_____

_____

_____

_____

_____

"You should never regret anything in life. If it's good, it's wonderful. If it's bad, it's an experience" – Unknown

Day 22

The Let-Down

Think about the times when you felt let down by a loved one. When was this? How did you feel at that moment? How do you feel about it now? If it's still as powerful and hurtful, why? Why do you think you cannot go over it? Are your feelings rational? Or are you maybe exaggerating? Stand in that person's shoes and think about how you would feel if you did that thing to them. Be brutally honest. Do you still feel that hurt?

_____

_____

_____

_____

_____

_____

_____

_____

_____

_____

_____

_____

_____

_____

_____

_____

_____

_____

_____

_____

_____
_____
_____
_____
_____
_____
_____
_____
_____
_____
_____
_____
_____
_____
_____
_____
_____
_____
_____
_____
_____
_____
_____
_____
_____
_____
_____
_____

"Expectation is the root of all heartache" – William Shakespeare

Day 23

The Void

Do you ever feel empty inside? Like there is a hole that you simply cannot fill? Why do you think that is? Think about the times when these feelings of emptiness appear, and try to analyze the situations. What triggers you to feel that way? Now, write down some healthy strategies that you believe might make you feel more whole. Can you start applying some of those today?

_____

_____

_____

_____

_____

_____

_____

_____

_____

_____

_____

_____

_____

_____

_____

_____

_____

_____

_____

_____

_____

"If you want to become full, let yourself be empty" – Lao Tzu

Day 24

The Failure

Try to define failure. What does this word mean to you? Why? What makes it so terrible? Have you ever been in a similar situation? If not, imagine yourself failing in front of everybody. Write down 3-5 things that you believe people would think of you in that situation. Now, write down just as many things that you would want people to think of you after failing.

_____

_____

_____

_____

_____

_____

_____

_____

_____

_____

_____

_____

_____

_____

_____

_____

_____

_____

_____

_____

_____

_____

_____

_____

_____

_____

_____

_____

_____

_____

_____

_____

_____

_____

_____

_____

_____

_____

_____

_____

_____

_____

_____

_____

_____

_____

_____

_____

_____

_____

_____

"A person who never made a mistake never tried anything new" – Albert Einstein

Day 25

The Support

Do you feel supported by your loved ones? If not, explain why. Has this always been the case? How did you feel as a child? Were you able to count on the support of your parents/caregivers then? Is there anybody in your life you can count on? Write it down, along with how you can rely on them. Think about always having someone on your side, no matter what. How does it feel to be always protected?

_____

_____

_____

_____

_____

_____

_____

_____

_____

_____

_____

_____

_____

_____

_____

_____

_____

_____

_____

_____

_____

"Support yourself and heaven will help you" – Senegalese proverb

Day 26

The Overreact

We all overreact sometimes. That is just our shadow trying to express itself when we don't know how. Think about the last time you seriously overreacted. Why did you act that way? Explain the situation here and try to pinpoint what thoughts and beliefs caused it to happen. How did that make you feel? If you overreacted in a conversation with another person, how do you think the other person felt? Imagine talking to them and try to rationalize the situation. What would you say?

_____

_____

_____

_____

_____

_____

_____

_____

_____

_____

_____

_____

_____

_____

_____

_____

_____

_____

_____

_____

_____

_____

"It felt like the world, but it was probably nothing" – a spun Morrissey quote

Day 27

The Grudge

Do you hold a grudge against someone? Why? What has happened for you to be feeling this way? Explain. Now, think about this situation but from the other point of view. Think about it as the person you're holding a grudge against. Would they feel the same about you? How would that make you feel? Would you be hurt?

_____

_____

_____

_____

_____

_____

_____

_____

_____

_____

_____

_____

_____

_____

_____

_____

_____

_____

_____

_____

_____

_____

_____

_____

_____

_____
_____
_____
_____
_____
_____
_____
_____
_____
_____
_____
_____
_____
_____
_____
_____
_____
_____
_____
_____
_____
_____
_____
_____
_____
_____
_____
_____
_____

"Holding a grudge is like letting someone to live rent-free in your head" – Unknown

Day 28

The Conflict

When you find yourself in conflict with someone, how do you react? Do conflicts make you feel uncomfortable or do you love to speak your mind and make your point? Think about a recent conflict you've had with someone. Why did it happen? How was it resolved? Did you contribute to the resolve? Or were you the stubborn one?

_____

_____

_____

_____

_____

_____

_____

_____

_____

_____

_____

_____

_____

_____

_____

_____

_____

_____

_____

_____

_____

_____

_____
_____
_____
_____
_____
_____
_____
_____
_____
_____
_____
_____
_____
_____
_____
_____
_____
_____
_____
_____
_____
_____
_____
_____
_____
_____
_____

"It is more rewarding to resolve a conflict than to dissolve a relationship" – Josh McDowell

Day 29

The Priority

What are your priorities in your life? Write down the first 5-7 things that come to your mind. Are you on that list? When was the last time that you put yourself first? Do you practice self-care? If the answer is so-so, how do you think you can improve this? Would that jeopardize your other priorities? Try to come up with a schedule, solution where you allow yourself to be important. Because you are!

_____

_____

_____

_____

_____

_____

_____

_____

_____

_____

_____

_____

_____

_____

_____

_____

_____

_____

_____

"Make yourself a priority. Fill yourself up so that you can give more to others" – Oprah Winfrey

Day 30

The Hero

What is your idea of a hero? Do you have any (from real life, obviously)? What are the things you admire the most about them? Why do you think you ascribe them such positive traits? Do you have some of these traits? If not, could it be that you subconsciously wish to? Try to go through each of these traits and write a sentence on how you can start incorporating them into your own story. For instance, if "courageous" was on that list, your incorporation could be "I can finally share my big work idea with my boss without the fear of getting turned down."

_____

_____

_____

_____

_____

_____

_____

_____

_____

_____

_____

_____

_____

_____

_____

_____

_____

_____

_____
_____
_____
_____
_____
_____
_____
_____
_____
_____
_____
_____
_____
_____
_____
_____
_____
_____
_____
_____
_____
_____
_____
_____
_____
_____
_____
_____

"Be the kind of person that your heroes would be proud of" – Unknown

Day 31

The Promises We Keep (And Break)

Think about a promise you made that was so hard to keep, but you somehow managed to live up to expectations. Now think about another one that you broke. Why couldn't you stick to your word like in the first example? What was different this time around? How did this make the person who you let down feel? How did you feel? Did you do your best to uphold it? Would you do anything differently now?

_____

_____

_____

_____

_____

_____

_____

_____

_____

_____

_____

_____

_____

_____

_____

_____

_____

_____

_____

_____

_____

_____

_____

_____

_____

_____

_____

_____

_____

_____

_____

_____

_____

_____

_____

_____

_____

_____

_____

_____

_____

_____

_____

_____

_____

_____

_____

_____

_____

_____

"It is bad to break a promise, but it is even worse to let a promise break you" – Jennifer Donnely

Day 32

The Angry Bird

What makes you really angry? Think about it. What is it that pushes your buttons? If you cannot come up with a good answer, then try to explain the last time you felt truly angry at something or someone. What was your anger about? Try to write down the thoughts and emotions that you experienced during that time. Now, think about how you felt when that outburst passed. Couldn't you resolve things more calmly and felt that way the whole time?

_____

_____

_____

_____

_____

_____

_____

_____

_____

_____

_____

_____

_____

_____

_____

_____

_____

_____

_____

_____

_____

_____

_____

_____

_____

_____

_____

_____

_____

_____

_____

_____

_____

_____

_____

_____

_____

_____

_____

_____

_____

_____

_____

_____

_____

"For every minute you are angry, you lose sixty seconds of happiness" – Ralph Waldo Emerson

Day 33

The Hold Back

You know how we always think of the right things to say after the fight is over? Do you often feel like that? Do you fail to express your feelings at the right time? Think of a situation when your emotions were late to the party. Why do you think that happened? Were you afraid to share them with other people? Were you afraid to be misunderstood?

_____

_____

_____

_____

_____

_____

_____

_____

_____

_____

_____

_____

_____

_____

_____

_____

_____

_____

_____

_____

_____

_____
_____
_____
_____
_____
_____
_____
_____
_____
_____
_____
_____
_____
_____
_____
_____
_____
_____
_____
_____
_____
_____
_____
_____
_____
_____
_____
_____

"The things that you do not say tend to scream loudest within" – Beau Taplin

Day 34

The Failed Relationship

Think about a failed relationship from your past that hurt you the most. This can be with a partner, friend, or family member. Why did it end? It may hurt but write about the things you did wrong at that time. Would you do it all differently now? Have you moved on? Has the other person moved on? Now, think about all of the things you have learned from it. Talk briefly about the healthy relationships in your life now.

_____

_____

_____

_____

_____

_____

_____

_____

_____

_____

_____

_____

_____

_____

_____

_____

_____

_____

_____

_____

_____

_____

_____

_____

_____

_____

_____

_____

_____

_____

_____

_____

_____

_____

_____

_____

_____

_____

_____

_____

_____

_____

_____

_____

_____

"Every failed relationship is an opportunity for self-growth and learning. Be thankful, and simply move on!" – Unknown

Day 35

The Energy Drain

Have you ever been focused on something for so long and never seen tangible results? Explain that situation. Why have you allowed yourself to be sucked into such an energy-draining thought? What could you gain from the realization of this idea? Is there any other way to make that happen? What could you do that might give you similar results?

_____

_____

_____

_____

_____

_____

_____

_____

_____

_____

_____

_____

_____

_____

_____

_____

_____

_____

_____

_____

_____

_____

_____

_____

_____

_____

_____

_____

_____

_____

_____

_____

_____

_____

_____

_____

_____

_____

_____

_____

_____

_____

_____

_____

_____

_____

_____

_____

_____

_____

_____

"Hoping drains your energy. Acting creates energy!" – Robert Kiyosaki

Day 36

The Respect

Ask yourself this, and be honest – do you think that people respect you? If so, then who are these people? Why do you deserve their respect? Are there people who don't find you respectable? Why do you think that is? And finally, do you respect yourself? If you cannot quite answer that, ask yourself whether you are constantly seeking validations in others? If so, think about what you could do to be more comfortable with your choices and actions.

_____

_____

_____

_____

_____

_____

_____

_____

_____

_____

_____

_____

_____

_____

_____

_____

_____

_____

_____

_____

_____

"If you want to be respected, you must respect yourself" – proverb

Day 37

The Letter from Your Alter Ego

This is Brad Pitt calling for Edward Norton. Your shadow within trying to get in touch with your conscious self. Let it! Write down all of the things that your shadow self may have piled up inside, such as anger, fear, insecurity, pain… And then switch personalities. Pretend for a second that you have no care in the world. What does that feel like? Try to slay each negative feeling with an I-don't-care adjective. Next to "anger" write something like "carefree" or whatever it is that you think may be suitable. It surely is fun, isn't it?

_____

_____

_____

_____

_____

_____

_____

_____

_____

_____

_____

_____

_____

_____

_____

_____

_____

_____

_____

"One of the best feelings in the world is when you stop caring about the things that bothered you" – Unknown

Conclusion

Congratulations! You have just made it through the shadow! The ride was dark and bumpy, but with your conscious light that guided you along the way, you have finally understood why your negative self lurks in the dark.

My hope is that you've managed to light up the blackness within with these 37 demon-calling exercises. Just like you summoned that demon every single day for over a month, you should make it a practice to continue challenging your shadow daily.

Maybe it will be uncomfortable, maybe painful, but remember, whatever confusing or scary thing you encounter, it is not the situation that makes you afraid. It is the aspect of yourself you see in it. A dark projection of your shadow. And the only way to fight it is to practice shadow work. As Carl Jung said, shadow work is the path of the heart warrior! Happy self-discovering!

Thank You

"Happiness springs from doing good and helping others."
—Plato

Those who help others without any expectations in return experience more fulfillment, have higher levels of success, and live longer.

I want to create the opportunity for you to do this during this reading experience. For this, I have a very simple question... If it didn't cost you money, would you help someone you've never met before, even if you never got credit for it? If so, I want to ask for a favor on behalf of someone you do not know and likely never will. They are just like you and me, or perhaps how you were a few years ago...Less experienced, filled with the desire to help the world, seeking good information but not sure where to look...this is where you can help. The only way for us at Dreamlifepress to accomplish our mission of helping people on their spiritual growth journey is to first, reach them. And most people do judge a book by its reviews. So, if you have found this book helpful, would you please take a quick moment right now to leave an honest review of the book? It will cost you nothing and less than 60 seconds. Your review will help a stranger find this book and benefit from it.

One more person finds peace and happiness...one more person may find their passion in life...one more person experience a transformation that otherwise would never have happened...To make that come true, all you have to do is to leave a review. If you're on audible, click on the three dots in the top right of your screen, rate and review. If you're reading on a e-reader or kindle, just scroll to the bottom of the book, then swipe up and it will ask for a review. If this doesn't work, you can go to the book page on amazon or wherever store you purchased this from and leave a review from that page.

Scan these QR codes to leave a review on amazon

Amazon US   Amazon Uk

PS - If you feel good about helping an unknown person, you are my kind of people. I'm excited to continue helping you in your spiritual growth journey.

PPS - A little life hack - if you introduce something valuable to someone, they naturally associate that value to you. If you think this book can benefit anyone you know, send this book their way and build goodwill. From the bottom of my heart, thank you.

Your biggest fan – **Layla**